FOX CONTROL

Other books by Seán Frain and pubished by Swan Hill Press

The Pet Ferret Handbook

The Patterdale Terrier

The Traditional Working Terrier

FOX CONTROL

SEÁN FRAIN

SWAN·HILL PRESS

First published in the UK in 2006
by Swan Hill Quiller Press, an imprint of Quiller Publishing Ltd

British Library Cataloguing-in-Publication Data
A catalogue record for this book
is available from the British Library

ISBN 1 904057 81 0
     978 1 904057 81 9

Typeset by Phoenix Typesetting, Auldgirth, Dumfriesshire
Printed in England by Biddles Ltd, King's Lynn

Swan Hill Press

An imprint of Quiller Publishing Ltd
Wykey House, Wykey, Shrewsbury, SY4 1JA
Tel: 01939 261616 Fax: 01939 261606
E-mail: info@quillerbooks.com
Website: www.swanhillbooks.com

CONTENTS

This book is dedicated to the
memory of Jim Dalton

CHAPTER ONE

A HISTORY OF
THE HUNTED FOX

THE red fox (*Vulpes vulpes*) is an incredibly efficient predator and its antics in regard to the hunting of prey has meant that it has become one of the most hunted of all animals, not just in this country, but in several countries around the world. The ancient Egyptians, for instance, as well as the Arab nations round about, kept dogs that were more than capable of chasing and catching these wily creatures. Asia has long been an area of livestock keeping and birds such as chickens, that have been kept for eggs and meat over millenniums, and flocks of sheep, would need protecting from the predations of foxes and other killers such as lions and bears. King David of Israel is well known for his courage and the Bible records that he, on more than one occasion, fought off predators that were intent on carrying off his lambs. He killed lions and bears and he may well have taken the odd fox that chose his flock as a food source.

It wasn't just livestock, however, that was at risk. The eighteenth century naturalist, Hasslequist, tells of steps having to be taken to guard against losses of ripened grapes from raids by foxes. This was in the region of Bethlehem, but if grapes are eaten in one place by foxes, then one can be certain that the same holds true elsewhere. Foxes do indeed feed on fruit, and so one can well believe that this statement is, in fact, borne of reality. The Bible mentions foxes on a number of occasions and the book of Judges tells of three hundred foxes being caught by Samson, which he then used to burn the crops of the Philistines, the mortal enemies of God's people, by setting their brushes on fire and letting them loose into the fields, vineyards and olive groves. I wonder what the anti-hunting brigade would make of that!

Many people who are generally ignorant of the ways of foxes and

1

the countryside as a whole, imagine that man is being cruel and sadistic by hunting foxes using packs of hounds. In fact, these packs were simply filling in the void left by wolves, which no longer exist in the British countryside and in many other parts of the world too. Natural law makes it absolutely necessary for wolves to hunt in packs. Their general prey – deer, wild boar and so on – are well equipped to escape predators and they can so easily outclass any lone wolf. The idea of packing is simply to reduce the odds against success. For one wolf to catch a fox, for example, would mean odds of ninety-five per cent in favour of failure. But when wolves hunt as a pack, those odds are very much reduced, to around thirty, or, in some cases, even forty per cent in favour of success.

Wolves have become very cunning in their methods of hunting, simply because of the cunning of animals such as foxes that have learnt these ways simply because of being hunted. Let not man imagine that foxes show cunning due to being hunted by packs of hounds, for this behaviour was learnt long before, by a fox population which had to compete with packs of wolves for sustenance. Wolves undoubtedly hunt fox, but I suspect this is done more for the reason of reducing the competition, than for food, though wolves will indeed eat foxes when they make such a kill. A pack of wolves will hunt deer in the main and such hunts can drag on for days on end. The pack will watch for any sign of weakness and will eventually choose one of the herd they think they will successfully catch in time. The hunt is often very slow, walking pace for much of the time, but once the hunted animal has been selected, it is very difficult for that animal to shake off its pursuers. True, many hunts of this nature do fail, but quite a few succeed.

After six or seven days of trailing their quarry, they may simply walk the animal to such a state of fear and exhaustion that it simply lies down in the snow, or undergrowth, and awaits its inevitable end. At other times, because some of these animals may not be as weak as at first thought, the wolves have no choice but to attempt to split the hunted deer from the herd and drive it into the jaws of the awaiting wolves that have earlier split from the pack. And it is so easy for one of the deer to become separated from the rest of the herd. The best place to achieve this is in woodland. One of the herd may panic and suddenly take a left turn, when the others choose to go right. Once this split is accomplished, the odds for success at making a kill are much higher, though some do manage to find the herd again and escape. Very often, though, a few wolves will be waiting ahead and they will suddenly pounce on their prey and pull it down, at last enjoying a meal they have been in want of for the last week or so. It is such predators that have hunted the fox long before man began seeking out Reynard with his proud packs of hounds. In fact, these packs were not used for the hunting of foxes until more recent times.

Hounds have been primarily used for the hunting of deer and one often hears of outcries by animal rights folk who complain that deer hunts last for hours on end. They should try studying wolves and their incredibly long hunts on deer, for those by hounds are trivial in comparison; a few hours compared with six or seven days of hunting! Early kings set aside much land as royal forestry and this was done in order to preserve deer herds which were used to entertain the upper classes, particularly royalty, with the sentence of blinding, or even of death, being passed upon anyone found poaching on royal ground. These royal forests were very often not forests in real terms, but were open countryside consisting of pasture, woodland and, in many parts, especially in the north of England, large tracts of moorland, even mountain. These areas contained many poor communities; farm labourers and general dog's bodies by all accounts, and the temptation to poach deer and other game must have been very strong indeed. In those days, if one turned to poaching in order to survive the hardships of poverty, then one had to be resolved never to get caught doing so, though saying and accomplishing are two different things entirely. Indeed, many were caught in the act and several lives were lost, or, at best, eyes were burnt out, or limbs lopped off (the poaching of hares, for instance, could result in the loss of an arm, if caught in the act). A heavy price for an act of survival, and all in aid of the king, or queen, depending on who was reigning at the time, having their enjoyment out in the hunting field.

In an attempt to reduce poaching, a common problem where poverty exists, even in modern times, though some poaching is a very lucrative business and not just a means of survival, no commoner was allowed to own any sort of hound that could have been utilised for the taking of deer and other game. Even large dogs of any breed were targeted and their usefulness severely curtailed by having three of the toes cut off one forepaw. As you can imagine, a dog with such a disfigurement would find it impossible to catch rabbits, let alone pull down deer which are incredibly fast, agile animals, able to jump high fences without a problem and covering much ground rapidly and with seemingly little effort. These methods, however, were not enough for King John who later passed several more laws that would prevent poaching, such as having any large dog hamstrung.

What these large royal forests did was to provide rich hunting and breeding grounds for foxes, though wolves and professional bounty hunters still proved to be their worst enemies. Foxes, before the early part of the eighteenth century, were considered as vermin and all measures were taken, not only to control their numbers, but eradicate them from areas where they caused severe problems. During the reign of Elizabeth I an act of parliament was passed for the protection of grain which the nation depended upon. Any failure of a harvest would mean disaster for that year, until the following harvest could be gathered, and so measures were taken to aid the success of the agricultural industry, in spite of great difficulties. But what does this have to do with foxes? That same act also provided a bounty of twelve pence for the head of every fox, or badger, that was taken.

This undoubtedly provided a good income for professional bounty hunters, but why foxes should be hunted down in connection with the protection of grain, I do not know. Though I can understand the law requiring badgers to be hunted, for these will not only dig vast setts out in the middle of fields used for crop growing, but they will also roll in crops such as corn and completely flatten large areas in doing so. However, foxes prey on chickens, ducks, geese and lambs and this would undoubtedly have had something to do with such a law being passed. The only trouble with this system was that, when a bounty is put on the head of any animal, persecution, rather than responsible control, is the order of the day and foxes were indeed persecuted, almost into oblivion.

Even before this time, though, foxes were considered as vermin, due entirely to their ruthless predations, any that raided a farmyard, or took lambs from the lambing pastures, were hunted down until caught and killed. Very often though, several foxes would die before the culprit was caught, for it is true to say that not all foxes make a nuisance of themselves. Some do not take to raiding farm-yards and not all foxes get a taste for lamb. And so not all foxes deserved to die. In some cases, particularly through the nineteenth century, whole villages would turn out to help hunt down a fox that had taken livestock and many hunts in the Lake District at this time occurred because a fox had taken someone's prize gamecock, or some other livestock. A hunt from 1899 tells of a fox that had been stealing ducks and geese from a farm close to Windermere's shores.

The following hunt will be compared to that of a foxhunt by a pack of wolves and we will thus see from this how man, along with his hounds, is simply fulfilling a role that had disappeared with the extinction of the wolf centuries before. A fox had been regularly taking livestock from this farm and hounds were called in after at least a score of ducks and geese had been taken. Some claim that foxes will not take geese, but I can assure you that they do. One smallholder I knew of lost several to foxes and I found eleven of their carcasses, some of the parts still uneaten, scattered around a field close to where the crimes had been committed. So disregard animal sentimentalists who will try to mislead you with tales of foxes being chased off farms by geese. I do not dispute that this will, on occasion, occur, for young, inexperienced foxes just starting on a life of independence, will often find themselves out of their depth when attempting to take something as large as a goose, but an experienced fox will have no trouble when it comes to the killing of such livestock. A young fox, fresh out of the nest and getting a little too bold for its own good, has been known to be killed by an outraged goose that has trapped it inside an outbuilding and pecked it to death, an incident I have witnessed myself, but such happenings are rare and do not occur with regard to older, wiser, experienced members of the vulpine race.

This fox that was prowling on livestock during the late summer and early autumn of 1899 proved to be game indeed, for many geese were killed and taken, until, one morning, a few couple of hounds were taken to Skelghyll wood, where a cold drag was taken up by the experienced pack. The fox had been going about its own business, simply making a living, but all the time it would know of the risks involved, as, for centuries, wolves would hunt down foxes that had taken prey and were proving to be very effective competition indeed. Predators breed according to the availability of food and so the wolf, having a strong instinct, a compelling drive, to reproduce, would do its utmost to cut down on that competition. And so the farmer and the fell Huntsmen, together with hounds, in the eyes of the hunted fox, were simply acting in the same manner as would a pack of wolves. True, by this time, foxes had not been hunted in this country since the sixteenth century when wolves became extinct, but even so, since then, hounds and running dogs have filled the void left and so the same instincts of survival have been produced in each successive generation. Just as a pack of wolves would search for the fox who was taking livestock in their territory, so the fell pack hunted for their quarry among the high woodland at Skelghyll.

The hounds soon began to show signs of a warmer scent as their tails moved from side to side with added urgency, their noses drinking in the trail of their enemy. And then, Rally, Glory, Drummer and Cruel, a good bitch hound, began to speak, their haunting cry ringing out from the cluster of trees and trailing away across the exposed mountainside. The fox was then seen by a young follower as it left the wood and headed out onto open fell, now going at a cracking pace across the rough, rock-strewn hill. The Huntsman cheered his pack on and it wasn't long before they too emerged from the wood and began going out across the fellside where the view of proceedings could be followed much more easily. When quarry goes away from them, wolves have developed a system where they attempt to drive it into a few waiting pack members. This is especially effective where the hunting of deer is concerned, but not so effective with regard to foxes.

With deer, the wolves would attempt to split their quarry from the herd and drive it to others waiting ahead. With a fox, they are very often alone and thus much more difficult to drive towards other pack members. And so a different strategy would be used in this case. Having scented a fox lying in the wood, some would enter and seek where it lay skulking, while others waited on the outside, trying to fathom which way the quarry would run and hoping to stay ahead of it in readiness of ambush. Very often, though, Reynard would get away from all of its enemies and take to open country. A chase, or a hunt, would then ensue, with a few being successful, but the majority ending in failure, the ambush method being the most effective. Sometimes hounds do manage to drive a fox towards other pack members and Reynard is quickly 'chopped' before getting any great distance. This, however, is more by accident than design, and so hounds usually flush a fox and then hunt it, or the fox rises from its couch as it hears hounds approaching and heads off, leaving a scent that is then keenly followed. There are differences to the way hounds and wolves hunt, but the goal remains the same; that of catching the prey and ending its life.

Reynard now took to the high fells and the Coniston pack hunted their quarry on to the tops of Wansfell, going behind the plantation and on past Petts quarries. These workings contain many huge earths that foxes will use for sanctuary when hard pressed. The fact that this fox chose to carry on may indicate its confidence and strength at the time, for if it had gone to ground here then it was unlikely that a terrier would be entered. Terriers have been entered below ground at this quarry, even in more recent decades, but the risk of such a terrier becoming trapped in an undiggable spot was, and still is, very high indeed and so most foxes were given best when they earth'd at such an infamous place as this. The fox then took hounds through Red Screes and remained awhile in the Kirkstone area, keeping ahead of the pack by using every obstacle possible; flocks of sheep which graze on open fell throughout the year, the many stone walls which climb untidily up the fellsides and across the felltops, bracken beds, now turning to that distinct russet colour which gives so much camouflage to a hunted fox, rocky outcrops, crags and screes.

The fox was next seen by way of Hart Crag and it eventually came back to the spot from where the hunt had begun, through Lowwood and behind Hartsop Hall. Reynard was now tiring rapidly, having taken the pack on a long hunt that had covered quite some distance, over severe terrain, the most testing terrain in all of England. His tongue hung out and his brush trailed behind him, his strength ebbing rapidly. His instincts, however, drove him on and it was now thought that he was making for Dove Crag, a place where he would undoubtedly have been safe. Before he could reach such a fortress, though, hounds finally caught up with him and finished his life of crime in the beck at Dovedale. Of course, when taking livestock from a farmyard, or lambs from the pastures, a fox is only following its instincts to survive, but even so, severe losses such as had occurred to this particular farmer cannot be allowed to go on unpunished, just as a thief cannot be left to plunder the livelihoods of others unpunished. And so this particular chap must have been delighted when the pack caught up with the culprit at last. A pack of wolves would hunt a fox in order to ensure a good food supply for their pack, just as a Huntsman will hunt a fox in order to protect the living of the farmers in his hunt country. Of course, in England, Wales and Scotland, the hunting of foxes in the old traditional way, a way that works incredibly well, filling the void left by the absence of wolves, is now illegal and so other methods must be employed, methods which are not nearly as natural, but more of that later. It is interesting to note that the losses of livestock ended abruptly after this hunt and so the culprit had indeed been successfully dealt with.

Another hunt took place after four geese had been slaughtered by a prowling fox. The farmer found his geese at daybreak and called in the Eskdale and Ennerdale, which was then in the mastership of the famous Tommy Dobson, who also hunted the pack. It was a grey November morning in the year 1900 and hounds were taken to Birkby moor soon after dawn had broken. Hounds quickly picked up a drag and had their fox afoot, which then led them, as one would expect from a fell fox, through heather and rock, up hill and down dale, and then finally crossing a stubble field in the lowlands, where hounds checked. The fox had crossed the Esk river, resulting in scent being lost for a while, until Willie Porter at last spied his quarry as it headed back into the hills. The pack was holloa'd onto the line once more and the trail now led them to the crags at Linbeck Ghyll.

The fox had found itself quite a stronghold among the rocks here, but still, a terrier was entered, despite this being a difficult place. Remember, in the shires a fox is often given best when it enters a bad spot, but when a fox is guilty of taking livestock, especially in the fells where farmers and shepherds already have great difficulty in scraping a living, it must be dealt with. This large borran earth, or bield, was a challenging place for any terrier, but nevertheless Rose, a game bitch by any standards, took on the challenge and quickly found her enemy skulking among the twisted piles of rock and shale and mud. Reynard very often has the upper hand in such earths. For one thing, when a fox has been hunted, or chased to ground by lurchers, it is usually reluctant to bolt back out into the open, and with good reason, for it knows what awaits it outside. Another reason for this reluctance is that a fox knows when an earth is largely secure. If a place is shallow and easily diggable, a fox will usually bolt at the first opportunity, but if a den proves to be an impenetrable fortress, then shifting a skulking fox is difficult indeed. This is especially true if a terrier is of the stand off and bay, nip and tease, variety.

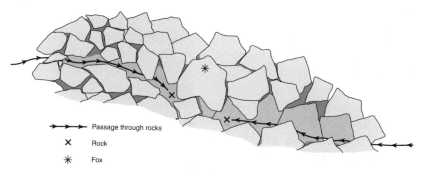

Passage through rocks
✕   Rock
✳   Fox

Foxes can sometimes get out of reach of a terrier and bolting them often proves impossible.

Not that there is anything wrong with such a terrier. They are fine where earths are diggable, but in the fell country where a fox will go to ground in huge piles of rocks several feet deep, one needs a harder terrier if a successful bolt, or indeed, a kill underground, is to be effected. Rose, the terrier now entered at Linbeck Ghyll, proved to be game indeed, for she worked her fox hard and eventually persuaded it to make for open fell, rather than remain below with that fighting fury. However, it wasn't long before hounds caught up with their quarry and ended its crimes. Four geese had perished and the culprit was dealt with in a most efficient and effective manner. Again, to that fox, it was being hunted down in order to eliminate the competition, just as wolves hunted its ancestors down for the same reason. A man's livelihood means his survival, just as a pack of wolves need a livelihood in the form of available food sources.

After the wolf, bounty hunters soon became a dreaded enemy of the fox. Before the invention of guns, foxes would be taken using terriers, running dogs and hounds and these bounty hunters would travel around large areas of countryside in search of their quarry, whether it be foxes, badgers, otters, or some other species they were paid to hunt down. Polecats and pine martens were also hunted down and any animal that had fur, which was in demand, was hunted with far more enthusiasm than were other less valuable species. The bounty and fur trade must have brought in quite a tidy sum for the more efficient hunters of early times, but still, it must have been a hard life, probably as hard as that of a drover who spent much of his time sleeping outdoors after long days of tramping across the countryside in all weathers. Inns would have been used and no doubt many farmers had a bed to spare for the bounty hunters working in their area, though this was probably among the hay in a barn.

They were hardy characters, for sure, but none more so than those who travelled throughout Scotland and who had the task of killing predators which preyed upon the crofter's stock. Later, when shoots became fashionable in Scotland, particularly during the Victorian era, these travelling hunters would take predators from such places in order to protect game. These travelling hunters became known as 'Todhunters' (Tod being another name for a fox), or, in the more remote glens, 'Brocaires'. Their task was to travel throughout the different districts and kill as many predators as was possible. Also, just like those who worked the fell packs of Cumberland, he was there to tackle any fox that was proving troublesome, not to mention badgers, or otters, as well as martens, or any other creature making a nuisance of themselves. One of these todhunters was called out when a Highland crofter had lost up to a score of geese to a marauding fox.

He had at his disposal a few couple of hounds and a brace or two of shaggy terriers of the nondescript type, though these were undoubtedly the ancestors to modern Scottish breeds. He sometimes had a lurcher by his side and he would usually carry a gun. Hounds took up the scent of this troublesome fox and trailed it to a large cairn (a naturally formed rockpile similar to those found in the Lake District, though often much larger). A terrier was loosed and the fox quickly found. These terriers which worked with todhunters, gamekeepers and crofters alike, were incredibly game and, because of having been native to the Highlands for centuries, had a canny

10

Isle of Skye where Todhunters once roamed, controlling fox numbers for crofters.

knack of working rock earths in particular. The terrier proved exceptionally game and Reynard bolted soon after, making for open mountain as it dodged through the rocks. The Todhunter took aim and fired, killing his fox instantly and ending its crimes, to the relief of the local crofters. It was a system that worked very well indeed, though some of these Todhunters became so good at their job that they almost wiped out the fox population in many areas. In fact, during the latter part of the nineteenth century, in the Dumfries and Galloway areas, one of these Todhunters boasted that he had indeed killed every fox in the district. True, he may not have been able to find any more foxes, but when an animal species declines to very low numbers, they are going to be far more difficult to find anyway. Also, they become far more shy and keep clear of man's dwellings and nature seems to kick in, as though the scent trail left behind fades very much, in order to aid recovery. So I do not believe that this man successfully killed every fox in his area. I believe numbers became so low that it was nigh on impossible to find one,

11

like looking for a needle in a haystack. And anyway, no animal, not even the dreaded rat, should be eliminated and, in my opinion, this todhunter should have been publicly flogged for his boasting!

Charles St John, a keen foxhunter who rode over the fields of Leicestershire for many years, before moving to eastern Scotland, tells us of these Todhunters who were to be found roaming the Scottish Highlands and glens, as well as the Borders and possibly as far south as Cumbria (I believe the terriers of the Highland foxhunters played an important part in the early development of the Fell terrier). In 1836 he wrote: 'Of all the ways of earning a living, perhaps there is none that requires a greater degree of hardihood and acuteness than that of the trade of a vermin killer in the Highlands – meaning by vermin not magpies, crows and such "small deer", but the stronger, wilder carnivorous natives of the mountains and forests – the enemies of sheep and lambs. In the Highlands he is honoured with the title of the foxhunter, or todhunter, but the Highland foxhunter leads a very different life and heads a very different establishment from him of Leicestershire. When you first come upon him in some wild glen, you are somewhat startled at his appearance and bearing. He is generally a wiry, active man, past middle age, slung round with pouches and belts for carrying the implements of his trade; he wears a huge cap of badger skin and carries an old fashioned, long barrelled fowling piece. At his feet follow two or three couple of strong, gaunt slowhounds, a brace of greyhounds, rough and with a good dash of the lurcher, and a miscellaneous tail of terriers of every degree.' This fascinating quote, taken from *Lurchers and Longdogs* by E.G. Walsh, gives us a rare insight into that most fascinating of characters, the Todhunter of the Scottish mountains.

He would have need to be wiry and active, considering that he both travelled and hunted entirely on foot, though there may have been some who utilised ponies, especially when covering the lowlands. His garb would be warm and weather resistant, for most of his work would have been carried out during the autumn, winter and early spring months when the weather can be severe to say the least, hence the need for a huge cap made from badger skin. A gun, during later centuries, would be most useful, for, although 'greyhounds' (possibly ancestors of Scottish deerhounds, descendants of the Celtic hound) and scenting hounds made up of much foxhound blood, are mentioned, much of the terrain of the Highlands would make it impossible to use running dogs. And so a gun, particularly in the more rocky and craggy regions, where using running dogs would be very dangerous and most unwise, would come in very handy indeed. Of course, nets would also be used, for catching bolting foxes from earths where it was possible to use them. At other times, the terriers would kill these foxes below ground, for they were incredibly game. Most terriers would then make their way back to the surface, while others would be too weak to get out, or they would become trapped, often forever. The Highlands of Scotland are one of the worst places on earth for working terriers and some of those rocky dens are fearsome spots. No doubt there were many places avoided by these Todhunters.

The quote also mentions that these terriers were of 'every degree', or, in other words, they were not of any fixed type. It is known that the ancestors of modern fox terriers were used by some of these Todhunters, for even Parson Jack Russell sent terriers over the Border and some were working with packs which covered hunt countries at the foot of the Highlands, during the nineteenth century, so they were certainly available to vermin controllers, but it was native stock that was used in the main. These, I believe, were undoubtedly descended from the Celtic terrier, which gave rise to the Highland terrier, which, in turn, gave rise to the modern pedigree Scottish breeds. The Highland terrier was quite a small type, ranging from ten to thirteen inches, with a very strong head, prick ears, a rough coat and quite a long back, though some were also short-coupled. They came in a range of different colours too, including white, black, black and tan, sandy and grey, and no doubt a few other shades too. But their main feature was their gameness. They literally feared nothing and very often they would rather die than give up, when working quarry. Tales abound of these terriers staying in earths until both fox and terrier had died. They faced badger and otter with equal enthusiasm, yet they also made excellent ratting and rabbiting terriers. They had a special ability when it came to working rock earths and undoubtedly this ability has been passed on to the fell strains that have been used throughout Cumbria for centuries. In fact, many of the early fell strains have a strong resemblance to working Scottish breeds of terrier of the nineteenth century, the prick ears and rough coat being just two of the features inherited from the Scottish earth dogs.

The skills learned by foxes in avoiding attacks by wolves later became invaluable when man began to hunt these beasts, not for sport, as became the fashion during the early part of the eighteenth century, but always as a means of controlling a predator that could inflict serious damage, damage that, in many cases, was impossible to recover from, to those whose livelihoods depended upon livestock. Terriers, running dogs and hounds were used in the fight to reduce numbers of foxes and those hounds used were very often from hunt kennels, though the pack was rarely employed in this capacity. The Holcombe Hunt is reputed to be the oldest pack of Harriers in the country and their quarry from the seventeenth century (and possibly much earlier) until 18 February 2005 when hunting was banned in England and Wales, has traditionally been the hare. But foxes have also been hunted.

The area surrounding Bury and Ramsbottom, the home of this pack, was mainly made up of royal forestry and sporting estates until more recent decades and it was on these country estates that the Holcombe hounds were employed. A few of these were used for flushing foxes from coverts to waiting running dogs, or, later on, guns, or, in some cases, the hounds successfully caught their quarry. Again, this was considered as vermin control. The fact that hounds, which traditionally hunted hare, could be used for flushing and sometimes hunting down foxes, gives us some insight into the actual numbers that were at one time found in our countryside. Numbers were very low indeed, due to terriers, lurchers, greyhounds, whippets ('rag' whippets were as game as terriers and they regularly took foxes, as well as large numbers of rabbits), nets, hounds and guns, not to mention snares and poisons, being used regularly against them. Litters of cubs, if discovered, were dug out and killed and the dog and vixen hunted down until caught. It was all out war against foxes and so there was little fear of hounds rioting on such quarry whilst hunting the more popular hare, for there were few around to riot on. However, hounds did sometimes put up a fox and these were very often hunted, long before the eighteenth century, but still, the fox remained as a verminous creature and it was always a disappointment when a fox, rather than a hare, was found.

If the sporting potential of foxes had not been widely discovered during the early part of the eighteenth century, then the fox population would be far fewer than it is today. True, the fox has been hunted, probably for thousands of years, even using hounds, but, as I have already stated, because it was considered as vermin and very often because a bounty was collected on each dead fox presented, not because of any ritualistic sporting practice. It is said that Thomas Boothby, a Leicestershire squire, was the first to begin appreciating the sporting qualities Reynard unwittingly possessed, in the year 1698. Others say that the second Duke of Buckingham, the master of the Bilsdale in North Yorkshire, was the first to hunt foxes for sport, rather than control, much earlier than Boothby. Which theory is correct is difficult to fathom, but one thing is certain; foxes had been hunted long before this time, though with far less seriousness and certainly with no 'science' involved. Often, if a fox was found, the whole village would turn out and surround the wood with dogs. The fox would then be dug out using a terrier and then turned loose, only to be savaged by the large, undisciplined pack of cur dogs. Sometimes nets would be placed around the wood, or a net placed over the hole, at other times the fox would be shot.

Before the beginning of the eighteenth century, hounds were often used to hunt all kinds of quarry anyway. Badgers, foxes, polecats, wildcats, stoats, deer and hare, were all on the quarry list, but the hare and deer were considered the real sporting quarries that were hunted with much more refinement and purpose. An extract from Nicholas Assheton's journal from June 1617, gives us a fascinating insight into the attitudes of some of these hunting folk of early times. First of all, note that this hunt took place in June, a time when hunted animals, unless they are causing problems, should be left strictly alone. The setting is the area now known as the Ribble Valley and the pack were kennelled at Downham, the village where the BBC's 'Born and Bred' drama is filmed. This extract is taken from Jane Ridley's interesting book, *Foxhunting*, and reads as follows: (24th June) 'To Worstow Brook. Tried for a foxe: found nothing. Towler lay at a rabbit, and wee stayed and wrought and took him. Home to Downham to a foot race.' (25th June) 'I hounded and killed a bitch foxe. After that to Salthill. There wee had a bowson (badger). Wee wrought him out and killed him.' Obviously some of these early sporting squires were not choosy about what, or when, they hunted!

As the seventeenth century drew to a close, attitudes were changing and many packs were gradually switching to the hunting of foxes alone, with hounds severely disciplined, or sometimes put down, if they proved intractable, for rioting on any other quarry species. And this is when fortunes began to change for the fox. One would hardly believe that this change could be for the better, but that is indeed the case. Prior to this, foxes were persecuted at every opportunity and numbers were very low indeed, right throughout the country, foxes being a rarity, almost non-existent in fact in some places. In areas where foxhunting took place on a serious basis, fox numbers now began to steadily increase, but if a pack was disbanded, the old ways of ridding the land of vermin returned and numbers sank dramatically once more, only recovering once a pack was reformed, or a neighbouring pack took over the country.

Where hounds hunted, a fund was set up that would compensate farmers who lost livestock to marauding foxes. Instead of Reynard being hunted down, hunts made payments in order that the culprit be left alone and measures such as these, together with the care and conservation of important coverts that included large tracts of woodland, ensured the prosperity of the fox population from then on. The large fox population now inhabiting the British Isles has come about simply because the hunting of this animal completely changed attitudes towards it. True, in some areas where mounted hunting could not be carried out, the fox has continued to be treated as the pest that it is, but even in these locations foxes are hunted on foot and so are not persecuted as severely as they were during former centuries.

When Parson Russell began getting together a pack of hounds after moving to a new parish, he met with villagers and farmers who were incredibly intolerant of foxes, due to the losses of livestock they had suffered. The villagers would turn out in great numbers in order to dig out and kill any foxes found in the area, including litters of cubs, but eventually the Parson changed these attitudes and folk began leaving them alone in order that they may be hunted. So we can conclude from these facts, that hunting foxes using hounds is actually a very good way to ensure a healthy population, both in numbers and actual health. Diseases such as mange and distemper are rife in some areas, especially in urban ones, but one finds far fewer health problems among foxes in those parts of the country that were formerly hunted using hounds.

This is because, when hounds hunt an area, they will catch sick and weak individuals and very often, infectious disease is nipped in the bud early on, preventing the occurrence of a bad outbreak. Also, elderly foxes are more prone to catching and spreading disease, yet hounds will usually kill off the old, leaving, at the end of the season, a healthy and strong population, with perhaps just a little more cunning too. It was the same when wolves hunted foxes throughout the British Isles. They too would take out the weak, the sick and the old, leaving behind healthy stock that would breed come springtime. Legion are the number of diseased foxes that hounds have killed and this can only be a good thing. Taking out the weak and the old is also important for maintaining a strong, healthy stock of foxes, for it is these that are far more prone to catching and spreading disease in the first place. When governments ban the hunting of hounds, they actually do the fox population a dreadful disservice, for hunting in this way is the most natural form and, in my opinion, the most effective for producing and maintaining strong, healthy stock. A diseased animal suffers great hardships and will often have to endure a long, lingering death, usually from starvation because of being too weak to hunt prey. When hounds come along and find such an animal, 'chopping' it quickly, it is a kindness to have put it out of its misery. Where the hunting of hounds is banned, more foxes will suffer from increasing outbreaks of diseases such as mange and distemper. Let us hope that rabies never enters the British countryside!

Hunting with hounds has been very popular for millenniums and several ancient civilisations engaged in this kind of pursuit, ever since it was discovered that some breeds of dog could stick to a trail for surprising distances. One of the earliest writings regarding scent hounds comes from the historian, Xenophon, which he records in *Cynegeticus*, and these words describe true hunting hounds that have become so popular throughout Britain. This quote also informs us that both the Greeks and the Romans used hounds in this way. He wrote: '. . . In hunting they ought soon to quit the beaten tracks, slanting their heads towards the ground, smelling at the tracks and drooping their heads downwards, and while they dart glances this way and that, and wag their tails, they should go forward in a body towards the lairs, making many deviations.' This would easily describe modern hunting with a pack of hounds sticking as one body to a hot scent. Xenophon was speaking of a method of taking hares that only gate netters employ in this country, that of driving hares into nets, only they did it with hounds, rather than lurchers. Could it be that the Romans introduced scent hounds into this country? I believe that the Celts were responsible for bringing true hunting hounds to Irish and British shores, much earlier than the time of the Roman invasion, though it is possible that there were already native dogs that hunted by scent. The Normans certainly brought hounds with them during their conquests, but scent dogs were already well established on these shores long before this time.

With a history such as this, with every tool at man's disposal having been used against them, and having endured millenniums of time of being hunted by wolves and then hounds, is it any wonder that the fox has become inextricably linked with cunning? And rightly so. Foxes are incredibly cunning creatures and all kinds of tricks are employed when one is being hunted. They obviously know all about scent. They will try every trick in the book in an attempt to leave as little a trail of scent as it is possible to do so. Water, wall tops, roads, plough, herds of cattle and flocks of sheep, all are used when a fox is being hunted. When scent is poor and the pack are struggling, they will casually make their way ahead of the pack with little, if any, urgency. I have even seen a fox attempting to catch a pheasant while it was actually being hunted.

I was out with hounds and they had flushed a fox from a steep hillside full of gorse. The day was sunny and warm in late September, and the fox casually made its way across that hill and into a large bracken bed, where it actually chased, and nearly caught, a cock pheasant, despite the pack being not far behind, hunting its line through the bracken. However, due to the warm and dry conditions, scent was terrible and the fox easily escaped. This sort of thing happens regularly and I have many times witnessed it for myself, so it is obvious they do know when scent is bad. How they know this, I have no idea, but know they do. Maybe it is something in the cry of hounds, or, indeed, the lack of it, that tells them scent is poor!

On the other hand, when scent is good, foxes fairly fly, putting as much ground 'twixt the oncoming pack and themselves as it is possible to do. A fox never hangs around on a good scenting day. Again, maybe it is the eager cry of hounds that enables them to know! One thing, however, is for certain; foxes are not easy to catch and a pack of hounds must possess good nose, strength, determination and stamina, if they are to succeed in catching a healthy fox that goes away from a covert. As I have already stated, much of this cunning has been learned from centuries of being hunted by wolves, as well as those intent on catching up with any fox that had raided livestock at a farm, or the back garden of a village house, or, indeed, from fields full of lambs.

This cunning, along with incredible powers of endurance whilst being hunted, means that foxes have become born survivors. One of their best tricks is to 'play dead'. Clapham in *Foxhunting On The Lakeland Fells* mentions this and I have seen such a thing for myself, as have others. One of the worst incidents surrounding this little trick of playing dead, was told to me a few years ago by someone who actually witnessed the incident. A fox had been marked to ground in a steep wooded hillside close to the estate where I grew up. A terrier was put in and soon found, baying strongly in the same spot for some time. The fox was obviously not going to bolt, so digging commenced and some time later they broke through to fox and terrier. The terrier had killed its opponent and the owner of the dog took up his prize proudly, putting it inside his coat in order to prevent the dogs from 'ragging' the carcass. Back in the van, on the way home, the fox suddenly sprang to life and savaged the poor chap's stomach before it could be secured and properly dispatched. Quite a number of stitches were needed, I believe.

I was out with my terrier, Ghyll, when he disappeared into an earth on the edge of a moor near Rochdale. Much of the country I cover has not been hunted with hounds for many years, so it is necessary to work both coverts and earths if foxes are to be successfully taken. If coverts are not disturbed, foxes will live above ground for most of the time and terrier work then becomes very infrequent indeed. And so I have always hunted terriers above and below ground, for maximum efficiency. The earth was a dug-out rabbit hole and I could hear Ghyll baying strongly. This was a one-holer and so a dig was on the cards, for Ghyll was an incredibly strong terrier, a little on the larger side, and a fox was not going to push past him! I took a reading on the locator and the depth was only around two feet.

I cut a two-foot square of turf, consisting of dense moorland grasses which made the task rather difficult, and began digging down to the sounds of barking, growling, bumping, hissing and spitting, eventually breaking through to my terrier who had throttled his fox. He held it tightly by the windpipe and squeezed all life out of his victim. I cleared around him and made enough space so that I could work and then reached over him and pulled out the dead fox. It was an average-sized adult dog fox and Ghyll had killed it in a very short space of time, for the dig had only lasted for a few minutes, the going being much easier once I had succeeded in removing the large square of turf. I managed to get Ghyll to leave his prey alone and I sat there looking at it. Suddenly, that fox jumped up and began running across the moor. Ghyll, fortunately, was still loose and was immediately in hot pursuit. His victim had been weakened considerably from the encounter and so the terrier quickly caught it again and pulled it down. I then dispatched it instantly and the fox was at last accounted for. It had been completely lifeless when I took it from that hole-end and even after Ghyll had released his grip, it continued lifeless for a time, obviously awaiting its chance. Some say that foxes go into a coma-like state when this sort of thing occurs, but I do not believe this to be so. I believe, once they know they have no chance against an opponent, they simply go limp, playing dead, in the hopes that their foe drops them and leaves them alone, thinking them dead. And then, when this has been accomplished, they choose their moment to attempt an escape. It is yet another side to the cunning of the vulpine race. Anyone who has hunted foxes for any length of time will be familiar with this cunning and my experiences in this regard are many indeed. I will record one or two of these incidents in order to demonstrate exactly how determined and cunning foxes can be.

On the edge of the moors not far from Rochdale in Lancashire, lies an old quarry that had not been worked for at least four decades. A large rockpile often holds foxes here and the farmer who lived closeby at the time, Mr Ashworth, regularly lost chickens

Derek Webster with Rocky and Rosie and a fox taken on the moors above Rochdale.

and geese to them. On more than one occasion, I found the remains of his stock outside, or near, this rockpile. He hated foxes with a passion, not just because of the loss of his livestock, but also because he had seen numbers of ground nesting birds dwindle rapidly due to a growing fox population that was preying upon the eggs, youngsters and the parent birds too. A pair of partridge had nested in the same spot for years, just across the hill from his farm, and it gave him great pleasure to watch them rearing their brood each springtime. However, because foxes had successfully raided the nest during the past couple of breeding seasons, they had given up altogether and no longer bothered coming. The same could also be said of skylarks, curlew and lapwing. And so I had promised to do my best to thin out the local fox population in order to give both his livestock, and wild birds, a chance.

I was out with my terrier bitch, Rock, and my lurcher, Merle, and I decided to check out this rockpile. I knew immediately I reached the piles of stones that Reynard was at home, for Rock flew to ground without any hesitation. Terriers sometimes know an earth is occupied before they even reach the entrance, scent must be that strong, and they seem to panic, making a run for the hole before their master can prevent them. That is the attitude Rock now took on as she disappeared before I had had a chance to even think about it. I stationed myself on top of the rocks and Merle stood by my side in keen anticipation, trembling with excitement as he stared down at the hole, waiting. This spot is incredibly deep and vast in area, so it took some time for my terrier to find, but find she did. When one considers that many of the Lakeland earths are vast, deep rock holes known as borrans, or bields, one can understand why fell hunters are so keen to have terriers that prove good finders. A fox could easily be missed by a mediocre terrier in such a massive fortress earth.

Rock was no mediocre terrier, however, and she eventually found her quarry which, having not been disturbed in any way and knowing nothing of the danger outside, decided to bolt, making no attempt to make a fight of it with the yapping terrier, but quickly getting out of there instead. The fox suddenly erupted from a gap between two huge slabs of stone, right at my feet, and Merle was quickly in action, though the going was very rough indeed and the fox slowly gained ground across the huge boulders. This is one thing I have noticed, when bolting foxes to waiting lurchers, or, indeed, hounds; they will choose the roughest and most difficult route, knowing that ground can usually be gained by doing so. No lurcher, or hound, is any match for a fox over rough country and this was plainly demonstrated now, as Merle vainly attempted to catch up with his prey among those rocks strewn everywhere.

One of the most effective demonstrations of the use of rough ground to escape a running dog was witnessed when I was out with my terrier, Ghyll, and a chap named Gary, who knew little, if anything, about the hunting of foxes. I had entered a couple of terriers for him and he was out with me one day as we hunted the area surrounding a sheep farm where I had been asked to control the often troublesome fox population. We tried a stone drain and Ghyll was quickly onto his fox, which refused to bolt. Ghyll would bay steadily, but if he could get a grip on the throat of his foe, it would soon perish. This fox was on guard, probably in a tight space, with little room to manoeuvre, and so Ghyll settled down, baying strongly and working close to his foe, awaiting his chance. I left Gary waiting outside the earth with the lurcher, while I headed off to the nearby farm for digging tackle. Shortly afterwards, the fox decided it was best to make for open ground and bolted, running across a footpath, with the lurcher close behind, and then heading for some rough, rocky ground full of large boulders and scree, in an attempt to throw off the lurcher. The clever ploy worked wonderfully and Reynard secured his brush. However, back to my original tale.

The fox came to the end of the rough country and was on much easier ground now, with Merle at last getting into his stride. He was quite a heavily built lurcher and so was not the fastest of dogs (he only ever caught one hare during the ten seasons he worked for me), but he was quicker than any fox on decent ground and that showed now. The fox must have felt his hot breath on its neck as he bore down on it relentlessly, but at the last minute it slipped betwixt two rocks and disappeared below. By this time, Rock had emerged and had joined in the chase. She was quickly into that hole and following her quarry eagerly, but I had reservations as to how successful she would be. I had worked this earth in the past, with absolutely no success. A terrier could get in at each end of this rock hole, but I had never known one get right through. My guess is that there is a large rock about the middle of the den and the fox jumps or climbs, onto this, out of reach of the terrier which cannot scale the smooth sides. Although I had had terriers to ground on foxes before this time, in this particular spot (this earth no longer exists, it was bulldozed shortly after this hunt when the quarry began being worked again), none had shown signs of ever having reached their prey. Rock had been at a fox in here on one earlier occasion, but she kept on emerging and running round to the other entrance, time and again, as though she couldn't quite reach her prey and was looking for another way of getting to it. She repeated this now, unable, once again, to get to the fox, which skulked safely inside, for, without a JCB, digging was out of the question. That fox had deliberately chosen the roughest route to that earth where it knew it would be safe, the rough ground buying it enough space and time to reach its goal. Reynard's cunning had once again won the day.

Another display of the determination to survive and of the cunning of foxes, was seen when Roy and I were hunting foxes for a shepherd who grazed his flock of sheep among the rough pastures at the foot of the western Pennines. This range of hills takes the full force of the bad weather coming off the Irish sea and it is a harsh landscape indeed. Foxes abound in this part of the country and livestock is taken on a fairly regular basis, especially at lambing time. It was for this reason that we were out after foxes that day, because lambs had been taken, though not in any great numbers. Even so, we wanted to stop the problem long before it got out of hand.

Three terriers, Rock, Pep and Judy, together with Bess, my greyhound, and Merle, the lurcher, accompanied us that day and they were loose, hunting around, as we crossed the fields, though being careful to stay well clear of the young lambs and those ewes which had yet to give birth. As we crossed a large field, a fox suddenly jumped out of a sparse growth of rushes and ran away at full speed, with Bess and Merle immediately giving chase and gaining ground rapidly. Just as the pair of running dogs were about to strike, the fox seemed to be suddenly swallowed up by the earth. The dogs stared into the mouth of a stone drain, marking eagerly. It wasn't long before the terriers were on the scene and all three made a bid to be first to the fox; disappearing into the darkness of the stone tunnel and scrambling along its length, desperate to catch up with the fleeing vulpine. I immediately began running to the exit hole at the bottom of the field, calling the two running dogs as I did so, in the hopes of getting there before the fox bolted.

There must have been a collapse around the middle of this drain, for the terriers could not get through, their wild, frustrated cries and their scratchings as they attempted to dig on, being easily audible at both ends. Merle then went away on a scent. The terriers, on realising that it was hopeless to try digging on, then emerged at the entrance and quickly joined me. They then shot into this hole and scrambled up the drain until they reached the other side of the blockage which, obviously, the fox had managed to get past. It had got through that drain rapidly, not hanging around for a second, for the scent Merle was now hunting was obviously that of our fleeing fox. It was as though it knew that the terriers were there and that it would not be safe if it remained in that drain, as though it only used it as a means of escaping the running dogs. I know this seems hard to believe, but there can be no other explanation for its actions. This was yet another demonstration of just how cunning foxes can be when being hunted, or chased.

We moved on, knowing we were beaten, and Merle began hunting around the reedbeds as we carried on through the fields, the terriers now coupled lest another fox jumps up. Merle showed interest at another spot, almost exactly the same as the last, just a small, isolated growth of rushes, and, sure enough, a second fox jumped out of its couch and began running across the field. It was too late to slip Bess, so I left Merle to his own devices. This time the fox began making straight for the farmyard. It made it to a stone wall just ahead of Merle and was quickly over, with Merle following. As it dropped onto the other side, however, it used the obstacles in that yard in order to dodge its pursuer. Again, the ploy worked and our fox escaped. We had already taken four foxes from this area that springtime so I was not too bothered about these escapees, but, again, I was amazed at the clever tactics foxes can employ when their life is in danger.

Another occasion was when I was out with Derek Webster, in the hills above Rochdale, on the edge of the 'Owd Bet's moors. The day was wet with drizzle and we had trudged around the many earths and likely 'bushing' spots all morning, with not a sign of a fox anywhere. There are some gorse bushes on Egerton moor, but I had only found rabbits lurking under the cover they afforded, and so I was not very hopeful, though there were one or two earths along this hillside where a fox may be found. We headed for the spot, but the earths were unoccupied, which was rather a disappointment. Again, we were in sheep rearing country and the shepherd required the fox population to be reduced in readiness of the forthcoming lambing season. Of course, I was happy to oblige.

Rocky, Derek's lurcher, is a superb all-rounder and he hunted around the gorse bushes, while the terriers, Mist and Fell, got into the thick of things. There was a decided shortage of rabbits here, yet Fell was showing keen interest at one particular dense gorse bush. Rocky seemed quite keen too, as he stood above, but, as the terrier entered, he dropped down off the hill and came round to the spot where the terrier had disappeared into the undergrowth. And then, above, at the spot where Rocky had been standing, a fox emerged and ran up the hill with great haste, finally disappearing onto the moor above. The terriers, alongside Rocky, were quickly up that hill and they went away rapidly on its scent, but it was too late. That fox had obviously seen Rocky above, while the terrier entered the bush below, where we stood, and the sides being overlooked by the lurcher. All exits were covered. Reynard was reluctant to make a move and was happy to dodge the terrier inside that dense, difficult place, until, that is, it saw its chance when Rocky moved. That split-second decision bought it enough time to put plenty of distance 'twixt hunter and hunted and again an escape was secured. Sometimes it can be a hard blow to take, when a fox secures its brush, but we shouldn't complain, for this is what makes them a formidable opponent – a worthy opponent.

One of the most cunning of tactics was seen when I was out with the Coniston Foxhounds one late winter day. The weather had been bitter cold, with a wind coming down from the Arctic, and snow lay on the tops of the fells, with some well covered for the most part, the snow becoming ribbed and then patchy until it finally gave out to the greens of the more fertile valleys below. That icy wind had calmed quite a bit, but still, the day was freezing cold, so I was well wrapped up. I had followed on foot for quite some distance, but hounds had been moved on to another dale and so I had returned to my car in order to keep up. A fox was found in woodland close to The Tongue, at Troutbeck Park, and hounds hunted it hard amongst the hills and dales, the woodland and forestry of this area.

As is often the case when hunting this sort of landscape, Reynard climbed into the hills, heading onto the High street range and making his way along the fellside in the direction of the valley head. I managed to pick him out using the binoculars and watched with great interest as he kept a good distance ahead of the oncoming pack, which followed his line keenly. Their voices baying into the cold afternoon air could clearly be heard and those haunting sounds stirred the soul of the foot and car followers alike. A terrific hunt then ensued, with a spectacular view being enjoyed as hunter and hunted remained on open fell. I watched as the fox made its way across incredibly steep, dangerous ghylls and waited for the pack to arrive at these obstacles. They carefully picked their course across the rocky ground and finally came out the other side, but with far less agility and skill than Reynard had shown.

Close to the head of the valley, Reynard began to climb higher and then, unbelievably, turned right and began running back from whence he came. I watched with great interest. Reynard was possibly fifty or so feet above the pack, but he could easily have been seen, were it not for the fact that hounds stuck to the line like glue, following by scent rather than sight, and so they missed their fox as it passed overhead. Hounds continued heading up the valley, while the fox was now rapidly running down the valley, back towards Troutbeck, its russet form standing out starkly against the mountainside ribbed with snow, the darkness of the rocks jutting out of the sea of white in places. At times, the fox crossed parts of the fell that were covered in deep virgin snow and the view of it was then even more spectacular. Although this was another display of cunning, that fox, a large dog fox, was eventually caught, on the hill opposite the village, after an extremely long hunt. Such hunts occur time and again in the fells.

To summarise, foxes have learnt their own particular art of survival from millenniums of being hunted, firstly by wolves and then vermin controllers such as Todhunters, alongside villagers and farmers themselves, who considered this animal to be nothing but a pest, a serious threat to their livelihoods. And then by hounds, after the sporting potential of the fox became the fashion during the early part of the eighteenth century. But even during this time, the fox's heyday, so to speak, when the population began to flourish after centuries of bitter persecution, due entirely to the preservation of stocks residing in hunt countries, after the scheme of compensating for livestock losses was adopted, Reynard continued to be treated as a pest and, in my opinion, rightly so. The fox is a predator, after all, so it should surprise no-one that his habits are going to clash more than a little with those who strive to make a living from livestock that can so easily fall prey to such an animal. Do not forget, it was after the hunting of foxes had become popular that the boom in the wool trade occurred, and so, because the fox will easily take lambs, and sometimes several at a time, this ensured that Reynard remains as a pest to farmers and shepherds alike, rather than a game sporting beast. Not that foxes should be persecuted. They are an integral part of the countryside and my wish is, with regard to my reasons for writing this book, that *responsible* fox control be carried out, in whatever form, rather than simply persecuting the animal until it becomes a rarity in some areas, as was the case during the nineteenth century.

Because the fox is such a cunning animal, if responsible control is to be effective, if you are to succeed in catching foxes in the first place, you need to know all about your quarry. This is the subject of the next chapter.

CHAPTER TWO

KNOWING YOUR QUARRY

THE fox family is a large and widespread one and it is well worth becoming more familiar with the different types, if we are to control this ruthless predator in an efficient way. We will deal with the red fox later, but first we will discuss the other members of this interesting dog family in order to aid us in knowing much about the background of these creatures. All, of course, are predators and all can prove troublesome as they act out the daily struggle to survive. Although foxes are not so different from dogs to warrant classing them as a separate subfamily, they are certainly 'different' in many ways and this will be discussed as the chapter progresses. Generally speaking, foxes have fairly long bodies, short legs, long muzzles with pointed noses and large, erect ears. They have long bushy tails known as brushes which are used to aid balance, and their pupils are oval shaped. Their coats vary quite considerably, depending on which country they inhabit.

North American red fox *(Vulpes fulva)*

This is very similar to its European cousin, but it is generally larger in size and its fur is longer, due, no doubt, to more severe winters. It lives on scrubland and the edge of forests and, like all foxes, is a master of survival. There are many varieties of colour in this species, including black, silver (black hairs tipped with white or grey) and a cross variety, which has a reddish pelt with black stripes. This type of fox is also hunted in America using hounds, terriers and the gun, but they can be quite difficult to catch as many will climb trees as readily as they will go to ground. Patterdale terriers are becoming ever more popular in America for working foxes, among other species, though Jack Russells and the more traditional Fell terriers are also used.

Grey fox *(Urocyon cinereoargenteus)*

This is found in most areas of the United States and southward into north South America. It lives in wooded areas and, like its red cousin, will very often climb trees, though it does live in dens dug into sandy banks. The grey fox has a black tipped tail, while all colour phases of the red fox have white tipped tails. Although mainly a haunter of forest and woodland, this fox has also been discovered inhabiting desert areas.

Arctic fox *(Alopex lagopus)*

When one talks about the incredible ability of foxes to survive, even when their seems to be both little food supplies and many enemies, this applies more to this species than to any other. They inhabit the tundra of Alaska and Greenland to northern Eurasia, where it feeds on a variety of prey, almost anything it can find that is even remotely edible. They are quite a bit smaller than an average-sized red fox and are a chocolate brown colour during the summer months when food is easier to come by, when cubs are reared, and turning white for the winter months, which aids them whilst hunting. In the snow they are not easily seen by their prey and thus kills are far more likely. Another phase is that of a smokey blue-grey which became very popular in the fur trade, fox farms being set up in order to breed for this attractive colouring which, after all, looks far better on a live animal, than in use as a fashion accessory! Actually catching food is difficult indeed for such animals, living where they live, but they will often feed on carrion and dead seals, or what is left of them, make up parts of their diet, along with fish, birds and even dead whales that are washed up. Arctic foxes will dig temporary burrows in the snow, but they will usually raise cubs in deep rocky laybrinths made up of volcanic rock, where they are very safe indeed. One would not wish to put a terrier into such places and even if one did, this fox is so small that few, if any, would reach them.

Kit fox *(Vulpes macrotis)*

Rather on the small side and it has larger ears than most others. It inhabits the deserts of parts of the United States and Mexico and is very shy. It is also a fast runner that can endure extreme desert heat, while needing little water. The larger ears will help it to cool down when hunting for prey, or when fleeing from enemies, in such heat.

Swift fox *(Vulpes velox)*

This is a close relative of the kit fox and is commonly associated with herds of bison. It no doubt feasts on the dead of these herds, for its numbers declined rapidly when the bison were all but wiped out.

Fennec fox *(Fennecus zerda)*

Yet another small fox with huge ears which inhabits dry desert regions in the main. It lives in North Africa and Arabia and feeds on rodents, birds, lizards and fruit, together with any carrion it comes across, though carrion does not last for long in the regions it hunts, so it is very competitive whilst searching for food. Fennec foxes are sociable creatures, but they do not thrive in colder areas. Again, the large ears are characteristic of foxes which live in a hot climate.

Other species

These include the African silver fox (*Vulpes chama*), a haunter of open sandy plains and another small fox, and the pale sand fox (*Vulpes pallida*) of the Sudan. Although such foxes do not do well in cold climates, they have a certain hardiness about them, for the desert regions can drop to severely cold temperatures during the night. And that just about covers the fox family, apart from the European variety of the red fox, giving us a glimpse into just how widespread they have become. Wherever they are found, foxes tend to thrive when food supplies are plentiful, though, where hunted for fur, or because they make a nuisance of themselves, they do not do nearly as well.

European red fox *(Vulpes vulpes)*

We will now concentrate on that member of the fox family that has been hunted in the British Isles for thousands of years, using a variety of different methods. This is such a striking and distinct animal that it is impossible to mistake them for something else. They are generally of a russet-red colour, which is at its best during the winter months, from October through to the early spring. They have white under parts and black on the lower part of their legs, with white, or silvery, tipped hairs around the rump. The underside of the brush, the name for a fox's tail, is usually black and is tipped

Fox scats.

with white. Some of these tips are large, while others are small, and on occasion a fox may be seen with no white tip at all, just a red brush. They have large erect ears and amber eyes with oval pupils. The lower part of the mask is white, as are the insides of the ears. A dog fox will stand at around fourteen inches at the shoulder and will weigh, on average, about fifteen pounds, though some are much heavier. Joe Bowman, during a hunt in the late 1890s, took three foxes in one day's hunting and all weighed in at over twenty pounds each. I have also dug foxes of a similar weight, though the majority will weigh around the average. Vixens are just slightly smaller and weigh a little less.

Diet, of course, has much to do with the weight of a fox. If the pickings are rich, then the bigger and heavier the foxes in that area will be. It is the same with rats. I often go ratting on keepered estates in order to cut down on the numbers which feed on the grain put out for pheasants, costing the estate quite a bit in lost revenue. Winter corn is usually grown too, in order to provide cover for the pheasants. This not only provides the beaters with cover to work, in order to flush birds to the waiting guns, but also aids them to avoid capture by predators. The only trouble is that this corn, along with the grain provided at 'feeders', means a steady supply of food throughout the winter. This means that rats will breed throughout the winter too. Inevitably, because there is a never-ending food supply at this time, the rats grow to enormous sizes and a ferret working such areas has its work cut out, I can tell you. In other areas, where food supplies are not so readily obtained, rats will cease breeding through the winter and will not usually reach such large sizes.

Foxes that are heaviest, I believe, usually come from hilly districts. But why should this have any bearing on foxes reaching larger than average sizes? It is because foxes are not only opportunistic hunters, but carrion eaters too. That is, they will eat dead flesh that may be even days old. They have stomachs of iron and so even partly rotting flesh will be tackled at times. In hilly districts, dead sheep make up an important part of the diet of moorland and mountain foxes and mutton is very fattening. Hence the reason why hill foxes can grow larger, and weigh more, than their lowland cousins. Dead sheep in the shires can so easily be found and removed by the farmer, but up on the hills, if a sheep dies in a remote, isolated spot, it is unlikely that discovery will occur, and so the dead animal is left to nature. Crows, rooks and magpies will, of course, get whatever they can, and it is usually the eyes that go first, while foxes and badgers will finish off the rest. On many, many occasions I have been out in the hills and come upon a dead sheep that has been stripped bare by foxes and badgers in that area. Well-worn pathways leading to and from the carcass betray the fact that these animals have been coming here on a regular basis for the last few nights, until there was nothing left to scrounge. True, some lowland foxes can grow to large sizes and reach heavy weights, but I will guarantee that this occurs far more so with hill foxes. Hence the reason for the legend of the 'greyhound' fox.

Many old reports of fellhunting in particular, will tell tales of greyhound foxes that once inhabited our mountainous regions. Old newspaper reports of some of Peel's hunts, say that the fox caught was of the greyhound variety, weighing in at sixteen pounds, or more. The same legend occurs in the Highlands of Scotland, and in many hilly districts, such as the Pennines. Is there, or was there, a separate race that could claim its own identity as a greyhound fox? One of the characteristics given is that this race of mountain fox was bigger than the average. As I have already explained, these larger sizes are very often due to the fact that dead sheep are left out on the fells and it is these that provide a fatty diet that enables foxes living off such meat to grow larger than the average. Many of these so-called greyhound foxes weighed in at sixteen pounds, which is only just above the average and many lowland specimens would easily tip the scales at that weight, and more. So there is little, if any, substance in this. Another characteristic given is that grey-hound foxes are leggier beasts. But is this really so?

There is some variance in both the weight and height of foxes and so there are going to be some that are leggier than others, but I believe it is the nature of the landscape that gives the fell fox a taller appearance. True, a good diet that includes mutton from dead sheep found on the fells, will enable a fox to grow to its full potential, in both height and weight, but a high country fox will be much leaner than a low country fox and this could account for the leggier appearance. Not that fell foxes are skinny beasts, veritable 'bags of bones', not in the slightest. Lowland foxes will very often have no need of travelling far, before a meal can be obtained. Fell foxes, on the other hand, will travel great distances. This means that, despite enjoying fatty foods such as mutton, they will not have an ounce of fat on them. But what they lack in fat, they make up for in sheer bulk. Fell foxes are often heavier because fat is quickly turned into muscle. They are, in fact, the 'power lifters' of the vulpine race.

Hill foxes will have need of travelling much further distances because food is not so readily available in this type of country. Carrion such as dead sheep, makes up quite a large part of the diet, though they will haunt the lower regions too, for the richer pickings, returning to the heights at daybreak. In the late summer and early autumn, fruit is enjoyed, such as blackberries and bilberries. Throughout the spring, summer and autumn, insects such as beetles are eaten and these are rich in proteins, which aids in the building and repair of muscle tissue. Rabbits feature prominently in any fox's diet, though fell foxes do not have such an abundant supply when compared to their cousins in the shires. A strong fell fox carrying plenty of bulk, but virtually no fat, will be far leaner than one from the shires that has an abundance of rich pickings, and such a fox will look leggier when running across a bleak, windswept landscape.

As we have seen, the theory of greyhound foxes being heavier, larger and leggier, has very little substance indeed, but yet more reasons are given for these beasts being a separate race of vulpines. It is said that the greyhound fox was largely grey in colour and that this made it distinct from its red lowland cousin. All red foxes now found on the fells, it is said, are descended from foxes that were imported due to very low numbers in the hills, diseases such as mange and distemper having all but wiped them out. I have seen one of these so-called greyhound foxes. It was mounted in a glass case and was caught by the Blencathra Foxhounds during the nineteenth century, when Squire Crozier was the Master. It was grey in colour, almost all over, true, but in no way different to many lowland foxes I have hunted.

One of these was in a rockpile at an old quarry. I was not hunting, but was simply out walking one cold winter day. I only had Rock with me and she entered the rocks as I walked nearby. There was something in the urgency of her stride that told me a fox was at home. Sure enough, she soon began baying and settled down in one spot, the fox refusing to budge. However, Rock was an incredibly game bitch and digs with her were hair-raising to say the least, for she would hurl herself at foxes and tackle them hard, no matter how furiously they retaliated. Her sire, Turk, a Lakeland type, owned by Dave Jones of Urmston, was a very hard dog and any fox that remained below would meet with certain death when he was put to ground, and I guess this is from where Rock had inherited her disposition.

Eventually, after Rock had tackled her quarry hard for twenty minutes or so, it decided to get out of there rather swiftly, bolting from the rocks only a few feet from where I stood. That fox was very grey in colour, yet it was not a fell fox, but a haunter of pasture and woodland. I have had many similar experiences, both in the high and in the low country, so this grey in the coat occurs throughout the fox population, even, I dare say, in the urban population too. I have no doubt that several mounted foxes can be found in Lakeland farmhouses that are said to be of the old 'greyhound' variety, but I have heard nothing, nor seen any evidence, that even suggests such foxes, a separate race to the lowland species, do exist, or ever have existed. In fact, if one looks at a typical fox, one will see that quite a bit of grey fleck exists in most specimens, particularly around the rump area and around the head. Foxes that are grey almost everywhere, with a faded red colouring underneath, simply have a larger occurrence of this natural feature.

Colouring, in fact, differs greatly in any fox population, whether it be high country, low country, or urban foxes; all will have variety of coloration and the hunter of foxes sees this variety all the more so. When hunting the fells in the old days and an unusually coloured fox was seen, its strength and cunning as it outwitted and outpaced the hounds much in evidence, one can easily understand how such a legend of a separate race of hardy and fleet foxes inhabiting the high country began, and grew, among the dwellers of the villages and farms of the fells. Such legends, as I have already stated, have also arisen in the Highlands and the Pennines, and no doubt in other mountainous and hilly regions, but, as we have seen, there is little, if any, substance in such legends. The more romantic among readers, however, may choose to continue believing such tales, despite the fact that they have been borne along with absolutely no hard evidence to go on. Having said this, it is possible that the grey colouring occurs more frequently in high country foxes, due, possibly, to the rocky terrain, and the rock earths, they hunt over and dwell in. If this is true, it simply means that the coat has become tinged with the colour of the landscape and earths they inhabit. It does not mean they are a separate race of a sort of 'super' fox.

One of the foxes I once hunted was almost black. We were rabbiting on a lowland farm and the terriers and lurchers were busy flushing bunnies from all kinds of cover, including gorse and bramble bushes. The runs around these places were well worn and they led to warrens on the hillside and around the field edges. Merle picked up a scent and followed it as it twisted and turned through the grass and into some rushes which grew all around a boggy patch at the bottom of a fairly steep hill. And then a rabbit suddenly shot out of the rush and grass covered bog and he was after it, snapping it up before it reached its warren. After the hillside had been well covered and every nook and cranny checked by the bobbery pack, we moved on into a small wood which grows on both sides of a deep cut valley by the side of a farm.

The undergrowth was very dense in here, but still, Barry and I were able to negotiate the place without too many problems. We found several half-eaten chickens in this wood and it was obvious a fox was using it. Whether the chickens were being taken from the farm situated closeby I do not know, but someone was suffering quite severe losses, judging by the carcasses we found that day. And then, as we approached the middle of the wood, Bess and Merle began circling a dense part of the undergrowth, while Pep, my Jack Russell, followed a run into the heart of this covert. She began barking furiously and the running dogs leapt about, looking out for any fleeing quarry. Suddenly, a fox, almost fully black in colour, came running out from the dense bushes and ran straight past me, with Bess and Merle now quickly on its brush and bearing down on it rapidly. That fox could no doubt feel their hot breath on it as they closed the gap, but it got into another dense covert just before they were close enough to strike. By the time they had made their way around to the other side, Reynard had disappeared in typical fashion, with hardly any scent left behind to betray the course he had taken.

Another fox I hunted had a large streak of black down the left

A stone drain under the ruins of an old mill.

side of its brush. I was hunting a wooded valley, which borders hill pastures where sheep are grazed. These fields were ploughed out of the moor centuries before and they needed plenty of tending and grazing in order to prevent the landscape reverting back to its once natural state. The farm lies surrounded by these pastures and, in the early spring, the flock is brought out of the hills in preparation for lambing time. During late March onwards, these fields echo to the sound of almost non-stop bleating as they become full to bursting with lambs. The bleating can be heard on the other side of the valley and is at its loudest throughout April when the flock has a continuous supply of newborns. Foxes, of course, will prey upon these lambs throughout the spring and so I was called upon to control the population in and around this area, in order to keep this predation to a minimum. This wasn't easy, for this is a difficult country to hunt, but still, I determined to make an effort and found that the best way of going about this was to disturb all of the coverts in that area and get the foxes going to ground.

Rock and Bella hunted through heather, bracken and bramble and on bracken hill they at last found a fox skulking among the ferns which were now turning to the warm russet colours of autumn. They barked eagerly and were obviously giving chase, but

I didn't see their quarry until it crossed the brook below and began the ascent of the hill opposite. As it followed a path upwards, heading towards the old mineshafts where it would be impossible to catch, I could clearly see the black streak running throughout the length of its brush, but only on one side. It made for an unusual sight. A few months later, I was hunting the same area when I saw a fox jump out of the heather and disappear into the cellars of a ruined mill.

I have worked this earth on many occasions and it is one of the biggest places I have ever come across. On occasion, if a terrier manages to chase its quarry into an offshoot of the main tunnel, which, incidentally, is big enough to allow a man access, then a dig is possible here, but usually there is little chance of actually catching a fox once it has got into this place. There are several ways of escape, which are impossible to cover. Most are impossible to cover with a net too. I had Merle with me that day, but he was by now in his tenth season and in the early stages of cancer, and so was of little use, if I am ruthlessly honest. Still, Rock had caught the scent of her foe and she now followed it below ground. She soon found and began baying furiously. A little later, the fox bolted from the main tunnel, but I was well away from there and Merle had no chance. Reynard then ran up the hill and I was amazed to see that it was the same fox with the large streak down the left side of its brush. It had eluded me yet again. Once more, it headed for the old mineshafts and I knew then that it was pointless going after it. Rock was certainly competent enough to work such a place, indeed, she bolted several foxes from that place over the years, but the holes are strewn across a large area of incredibly steep hillside and so actually catching a fox bolting from this earth is nigh on impossible. One can only watch helplessly as Reynard makes his way across country to some other residence where he will spend the daylight hours, until, with the sinking of the sun, it is time to begin his never-ending search for food once more.

The average size for the brush of a dog fox is around fifteen inches, slightly less for a vixen, but again, there is variety in sizes. For instance, some foxes have incredibly short brushes, only half the length in some cases. I was out walking my fell terrier bitch, Rock, only a few minutes from my home, when she caught the merest whiff of a scent and went off to investigate. She entered a large area of brambles, bracken and shrubbery. It was grey and drizzly and I expected any self-respecting fox to be deep inside its lair on such a dismal and damp day, but Rock began baying and then tangling with her quarry in the middle of the undergrowth and shortly afterwards a fox bolted out and ran across a marsh, before crossing the brook and heading up the other side of the valley. This fox had only a half-sized brush, without any white tip, yet I could see, as it fled rather rapidly, that it still used it in the same way as any other fox. The brush aids balance and is used to put in those incredibly quick turns that can make a fox difficult to catch for even the fleetest of lurchers.

Rock was off on its scent and she hunted it to the cut-out of an old, and long disused, railway line and followed its scent along the heather-clad banks, before, at last, she came to an unfathomable check and reluctantly returned to me. That fox had chosen to make a fight of it before fleeing and Rock had quite a nasty bite by the side of her eye, which I promptly treated on arriving home. The very next day, I was again walking my bitch when she disappeared into yet more dense undergrowth, working out the line of yet another scent. She began baying once more and shortly afterwards a fox bolted from cover. I heard it splash into the brook and then at last saw it as it climbed the bank on the other side and ran away up the hill, on more or less the same course as the previous day. It was the same fox too. The half-brush was clearly seen as it sped away, choosing not to make a fight of it this time! This covert was only twenty yards from the one it had laid up in during the previous day.

Whether these short brushes are natural features, or whether they are bitten off in fights when youngsters, I do not know, but I have come across a number of foxes with this disfigurement. One of these half-brushes was definitely a deformity the fox had been born with, for it came complete with the white tip, though others have no such natural markings and look as though they have been bitten off, probably as a cub. Chris, a friend of mine, was hunting the crags on a large moor situated on the edge of the western Pennines, when his terrier, Zak, marked a fox to ground in rocks close to the top. The terrier was entered and a hard, long dig then ensued. The fox had got itself into a tight spot and wasn't for moving, so Chris had no choice but to dig. This area is full of bad spots and any dig

A stone pipe used by foxes.

can be counted on to be difficult at best, impossible at worst. I have dug foxes on the lower slopes of this moor, in easily dug enlarged rabbit holes, but the higher slopes are inevitably rock spots and so actually accounting for a stubborn fox is not easy, to say the least.

However, Barry, another friend of mine and a one-time digging partner for several years, was out that day and he was a veritable human JCB. Where a fox was to ground and a terrier bayed, Barry would dig like a madman and only the most difficult of spots would prevent him from reaching his quarry. I have seen him dig virtual caves into a hillside when a terrier has been trapped to ground, so he was an asset to any team of diggers. Zak continued at his fox while the digging commenced and slowly progressed and tons of earth and rocks, some small others like boulders, were dug out of there. They dug into the hillside, only for about four or five feet,

41

but because of the nature of the terrain, it took time to progress even a few inches. Just cutting through the roots of heather for that first few inches, proved difficult enough, and rocks could only be pulled out once the impacted earth had been cleared from around them, the stones worked loose with the iron bar. However, in time, after a good couple of hours or so, Zak was finally reached and a space cleared around him. He was a hard terrier. A superb finder who, like my bitch Rock, had successfully worked some of the deepest earths in the Pennine hills. By the time the diggers unearthed him and his quarry, he had finished it. They pulled out the carcass of a small vixen, a rather poor specimen for a hill fox, and it had a brush about half the size of the normal, with the usual white tip, which told of it being born with this deformity. I was not there that day but Chris brought the carcass back with him, and he showed me the little vixen that evening. I would say she was the runt of the litter and had grown up a 'poor doer', as the saying goes in livestock circles, indicating an animal that just doesn't thrive. This was late November, so the vixen was fully grown by this time.

During the 1980s a fox with half a brush proved a real nuisance to the shepherds who grazed flocks among the high Pennines, for it had taken lambs, and been seen taking them, for a period of at least six years and several attempts at catching it had been made, without any success whatsoever. A shooting friend had hunted it for a number of years, attempting to call it in on the lamp, or waiting for it close to favourite haunts during the early morning and evening, but he too had had no success in catching up with it and ending its crimes. It was a big dog fox, that they knew from regular sightings (dog foxes have much broader heads and fuller bodies than vixens and are quite easy to distinguish), but had grown lamp-shy and very elusive, its cunning borne of both instinct and experience. The day I hunted that fox, for me anyway, was memorable indeed.

I had had a hard night of lamping for troublesome foxes, but had managed to get a couple of hours sleep before we set off into the hills while it was still dark. We were searching the high moors of the Pennines, which, at this time of year, were full of lambs. Some had been taken by foxes over recent weeks and, as usual, the fox with only half a brush was blamed. Probably eighty per cent of the kills were by other foxes, but, because this was the area this fox had

Drains are often used
by foxes.

An opening into a stone drain.

ranged over for the past six years or so, he would inevitably be blamed for every kill made, whether it be lamb, or farmyard fowl. We arrived as the pitch-blackness began to fade to a dull grey and set off onto the moors with a pack of lurchers and terriers. We would be trying every earth and every covert within miles of our starting point and I knew we were in for a hard day, especially when the clouds began to thin and disperse as the sun rose into the sky of a soft spring morning.

The first earth we came across was an incredibly long drain, which stretched out in an almost straight line, right across the moor. No foxes were found here, and no wonder. There were several breaks along the length of this drain where foxes had been dug out during several past hunts, some undoubtedly stretching back decades. The only trouble was, the hunters hadn't bothered back-filling and the drain had undoubtedly become so windblown and cold that no self-respecting fox would use it in the end. A local Huntsman had told me of how his hounds had put up a fox behind Holcombe hill, which lies on the edge of the western Pennines, and of how his pack had hunted it across the swell of hills until, at last, the quarry, unable to shake off the unrelenting pack, had sought sanctuary in an earth behind the Grey Mare Inn which stands exposed on top of this range of hills. They had then dug out the fox and dispatched it. The Huntsman has the mask and brush of this game fox on his living room wall. I wondered if this drain was the earth from where they had dug it. Whether it was, or otherwise, one thing was certain no fox was using it today, that is for sure, so we moved on, the pack of eager dogs hunting through reed beds and tracts of bracken, or deep heather.

As the sun rose higher into an ever-increasing blue sky, the walk across those high moors became harder and harder, until, by late morning, I felt utterly exhausted. Not only had we failed to find the fox with half a brush, but we failed to find any fox at all. So we gave up in the end, thoroughly beaten. As far as I know, that fox was never seen again and no hunter accounted for him either, that much I do know, so I guess he simply died of old age inside a remote earth out on those wild, exposed hills. He had lived a violent life and had come close to being caught on many occasions, but in the end he eluded all who sought him and died a peaceful death in his natural wild state.

Different coloured foxes

Foxes sometimes come in different colours. Albinos are rare, true, but white foxes are slightly more common. When I say white foxes, I do not mean typical albinos, for a true albino has pink eyes and almost pure white fur. White foxes have the usual amber eyes and often have other colouring too, such as black, or grey, flecks in the fur. A white fox had made quite a name for itself during the late 1960s as it evaded capture for several years, while being hunted by the Ullswater Foxhounds, then hunted by Joe Wear. After the meet at a local farm, hounds drew around the fells for quite some distance, but without finding a single fox. They had undoubtedly disturbed at least one fox, but its scent was not picked up, for it was seen above on Birkfellside, as they stood by the lakeside, wondering where next to draw. The fox seen was that elusive white vixen that had been hunted on several occasions prior to this. She had proved both cunning and fleet and had secured her brush every time. The followers and hunt servants were hoping to catch up with her on this occasion.

Hounds were taken up the fell and the white vixen soon spotted them as they made their way towards her. She turned and fled

A brick-lined drain that often holds foxes.

without delay. Hounds picked up her scent and went away, their music swelling as they stuck to the line eagerly, expertly, hungrily drinking in the hot musty taint of their age-old enemy. She dropped below the brow of the fell and followed a narrow and dangerous sheep trod to Kilbert How, eventually making for Lang Crag. 'Lang' is a Cumbrian term for 'long', so you can imagine how much ground the fox was able to gain on the pack over this incredibly rough country as she negotiated, with far more agility, this 'long' crag. She now climbed a sheer crag face and then made for Scale How wood. In the meantime, hounds had checked and were finding it difficult to fathom exactly which route the white fox had taken and eventually, after a slowly fading scent as they crossed the rough rocky ground, they lost the line completely. However, the vixen had been seen entering the wood by a follower and so hounds were taken there in order to make a cast, to see if they could find the line once more. Hounds went through the wood and picked up the line at Pearson Fold, the same line they had lost a little earlier. The hunt then became long and hard, yet hounds stuck to their task with real determination as the vixen led them back to where the hunt had begun.

The vixen disappeared from view as the hunt continued above Ullswater lake and hounds eventually followed her to Blowick woods, where scent twisted and turned through the trees as the vixen attempted to throw hounds off her trail. And then she left the cover of the trees, now running across lowland pastures to Side Farm, where the meet had been held that morning. She then hid in a garden at Patterdale village and hounds eventually flushed her from there, now hunting her through the gardens until almost the whole village was joining in the chase. She eventually fled and attempted to climb Placefell, but was too exhausted to make it, finally being caught by hounds as she made again for the lowlands. She had proven a game fox and was so revered that Christopher Ogilvie, the one-time Huntsman of the Coniston pack, composed a song to commemorate her capture.

White foxes are not exactly rare, though they are far from common. Derek Webster once caught a 'blond' fox, a colouring that results from a mix of white and slightly red fur. I have seen one of these before, though not live, for the mask and brush was hung over the mantlepiece of the fireplace of Dave Jones of Urmston. If

Derek Webster with a blond fox taken in North Wales.

I remember correctly, he had dug this fox with his bitch, Sally, the dam of my bitch, Rock, and daughter of Pip, an incredibly game fell type of terrier that was owned and worked by a chap in Rochdale; a terrier descended from the dogs bred by Frank Buck and Cyril Breay of North Yorkshire and Cumbria. Many of these Patterdale terriers were bought from both Buck and Breay and were worked in and around Rochdale, Oldham and the Rossendale valley, so few terriers around these districts, particularly during the 60s, 70s and 80s, were not bred from these terriers; earth dogs of superlative finding qualities.

Sally, too, proved a game terrier that could find foxes in the deepest of earths. Dave often worked his small team of terriers up in the Derbyshire hills and one day, while working around the Blue John mines area, Sally went to ground in a two-holed earth. Some

47

of the earths in and around Derbyshire are incredibly deep, difficult places to work and some are deadly. This earth, however, was fairly straight forward and Sally soon bottled up her fox in the stop-end. She was not a hard bitch. Like many Buck/Breay terriers, she had plenty of Border terrier in her lines and so she worked hard, but with plenty of sense which kept her out of trouble. She was, in fact, the perfect type for digging to. Digging commenced, but the going was difficult, for even straight-forward earths, particularly in hill country, can be hard to dig, due to roots, stones and shale, and whatever else is found while one digs down. I have come across all sorts of things while digging; sheets of tin and iron, bed springs, medicine bottles, drinks bottles, iron bars, builders' rubble, parts of cars, tyres etc, to name but a few.

Digging continued for a good three hours until, finally, Dave uncovered his bitch. She had worked close to her fox and had received a few minor bites, but she was none the worse and she continued at her quarry while the soil was cleared from around her. The fox was uncovered and proved to be of the 'blond', or sandy variety. Dave also had the mask of a sandy coloured badger on his wall, which he had dug during those days when it was legal to do so.

Derek Webster was hunting in North Wales when his lurcher, Rocky, showed keen interest at a large bramble thicket. Rocky then entered the covert and flushed a fox. He gave chase and eventually caught it and it proved to be a 'blond', or sandy fox. As I have stated, this colouring undoubtedly results from a mix of white and pale red fur. Again, this is not a common colouring found in foxes, though it is not nearly as rare as an albino. Whatever the colouring of a fox, one thing is certain – they are unmistakable when seen at a reasonable distance. Caught out of the corner of the eye, some cats can be mistaken for foxes, even some dogs can be mistaken too (a dog on my estate looks very similar to a fox at a distance), but when one gets a clear view, there is no room for such mistakes. The dense russet fur, the erect ears, the long brush and the cat-like movement, rather than dog-like, are unmistakable.

Habitation and diet

Foxes are literally found anywhere. They inhabit the highest of mountains and the lowest of lowlands. They are as common, and

Typical places to find foxes below ground, though they spend much of their time above ground.

probably more common in fact, in our city streets, as they are in the countryside and are born survivors. They have such a wide ranging diet that they can adapt to all kinds of situations and still manage to come out on top. They are natural scavengers and eat carrion just as eagerly as freshly caught meat. Like most predators, foxes will 'cache', or bury, much of their food and this is then dug up and eaten at a later date, when other food sources are not so easily found. The only trouble is, foxes seem to forget where they have buried food for much of the time and it often goes unclaimed. I am not convinced, though, that they actually do forget where their store of food is buried. Food is 'cached' for times when the fox fails to make a kill, ensuring their survival until the next meal is obtained. However, if a fox successfully kills for many days after food has been buried, then that stored meal will not be needed, and so the fox simply does not return to claim its prize, eventually forgetting about it, or instinctively knowing that, by this time, the meat will not be fit for consumption anyway. True, foxes will tackle meat that is far from its best, but there are limits!

Foxes will dig up their meat and will hold it very gingerly between their teeth while they shake off as much of the soil as possible. They will then tackle it with some soil still attached, but

49

with the majority cleaned off. Some wonder if other foxes watch while another buries its food, for foxes will often steal another's 'cached' meat. I think it unlikely. If you watch a fox burying food, it will often be a little careless whilst doing so. Part of the meat may remain unburied, or it will be buried very shallow indeed. A passing fox has a very sensitive nose and has no problems smelling food that is only partially, or only shallowly, buried. Foxes are opportunistic hunters, a quality that makes them born survivors in the first place, and they will not miss out on an easy meal, provided the meat is not too rotten. A fox that is seemingly stealing the buried prey of another, is simply acting on its instinct to take every opportunity that comes its way; a quality that will ensure survival through even the toughest of winters.

The fox enjoys great variety in its diet, though the staple part of its diet is probably rabbits. When myxomatosis decimated the rabbit population during the 1950s, some foxes struggled to survive, while others simply starved to death. In areas where recovery means that rabbits are once again found in large numbers, foxes will prey regularly on these creatures. Where rabbits are decimated by outbreaks of myxomatosis and the viral disease, VHD, in these modern times, foxes do not suffer the same hardships. Every fox in the district will visit an area full of diseased rabbits and then, when the supply has been exhausted and the disease outbreak has done its worst, they will simply disperse and head off back to their own territory, without the threat of starvation they once faced. This is because, back in the early 50s, Britain was far more rural and towns and cities far less built-up. Country foxes thus faced very difficult times when their most prominent food source disappeared almost overnight. During this horrendous time, about 95 per cent of the rabbit population was wiped out by that first outbreak, resulting in the decline of, not only foxes, but also buzzards and other predators such as stoats, though this was not only due to starvation because of a lack of available prey.

Predators will breed according to the availability of food and so few vixens will have given birth to cubs where food was scarce. Once they began to adapt and the weak and the old had simply died of starvation, then breeding would begin to get into full swing again, but not in those areas where survival was nigh on impossible. Litters that were born would undoubtedly have contained low numbers until food sources began to stabilise once more. Nowadays, with towns and cities encroaching ever more into country areas, the fox, if outbreaks of myxomatosis do their worst with local rabbit populations, simply lives a sort of double life, hunting both country districts, and the streets of our towns and cities for food. And there are plenty of food sources on our streets that are available to any country fox that occasionally enjoys sampling the 'bright lights', but more of that in another chapter.

In some ways, foxes are a friend of both the farmer and the game-keeper. In fact, if it were not for his ruthless ways when it comes to the killing of fowl and lambs, he would be a veritable ally, for foxes will prey on rabbits, rats and small rodents such as field mice, which can be a real nuisance to the farmer. Rabbits, for instance, while they benefit the land when found in modest numbers, due to their cropping the grass low and thus allowing low growing plants to thrive that attract insects and thus benefit the bird population, also cause great damage when found in high numbers. They dig up and scratch the land that is ruined in large areas, quickly becoming unsuited for grazing cattle, or sheep. Also, their urine and droppings kill vegetation when abundant. They will dig burrows in the middle of fields and horses, sheep and cattle can easily break their legs when they fall into them. They will eat crops as readily as they will tackle grass and this makes them a pest to crop-growing farmers. So on the surface, predators such as foxes seem a blessing to the farmer.

Rats, of course, will frequent farms and where feed, or crops are stored, they will multiply rapidly due to an abundant food source and can become so numerous that they end up costing a farmer thousands in lost feed and crops. Also, because they gnaw and dig almost constantly, when they are not feeding, they can undermine farm buildings to such an extent that demolition is the only answer. Rats will also consume very large quantities of feed put out for pheasants by keepers. Foxes prey on rats and where rabbits have been wiped out by disease, rats become a far more important food source. Like rats, mice will also eat crops and stored feed and they too can be a nuisance, hence the reason for most farms having a cat or two around the place. Mice though, are far less of a problem than rats and far fewer will be caught by foxes, though owls and other birds of prey will do a good job of tackling these small rodents. The traditional barn, where most feed was stored at one time, always held a pair of owls and these would prey on rats and mice inhabiting the same area. It is bad for both the farmer and the owl population that the traditional barn is slowly disappearing from our countryside. Let's have a 'save our traditional barns' campaign and see a return to old values and more environmentally friendly farming practices that benefit our wildlife. Again, if it were not for the thieving ways of foxes, in many ways he would be an asset to the farmer.

Although rabbit will make up a large part of the diet of foxes, they will prey on a variety of different species. As we have seen, rats and mice, as well as other small rodents, make up an important part of the diet of foxes. Watching a fox stalk voles, or mice, squabbling over territory among the tangled grasses makes for a fascinating scene. They use a combination of sight, scent and hearing for this task and one will see the keen, alert eyes scanning the grass all around, the nose twitching as it tests for scent that will give away the presence of prey, the ears moving in all directions in order to capture every sound, no matter how low, in order to pinpoint the exact whereabouts of the two combatants. And then, when Reynard has picked his spot, after being as still as a statue for a moment or two, he will suddenly leap into the air and come crashing down forepaws first, in an attempt to pin the prey to the ground. Great patience is exercised while carrying out this effective procedure and that patience usually pays off, though, of course, not always.

Rats are very often dug out of their warrens, or caught whilst out feeding, for they do not have the best eyesight in the world and a patient fox, if it stalks slowly and silently, will usually get within striking distance before being seen. On the whole, rats feed at night and foxes will chase them among the crops and hedgerows. But because rats are such prolific breeders, and they will breed all year round where food supplies are constant and abundant, this makes very little difference to actual numbers. Whole families of rats are sometimes dug out by a hunting fox, for a doe will not usually leave her youngsters, especially if they are helpless, blind and naked in the nest.

Hedgehogs are also preyed upon, but these can be a real challenge to a fox that has not been taught by a more experienced family member exactly how to go about killing them and getting to the meat. Young and inexperienced foxes will usually attempt to bite the spines and they become quickly frustrated when they realise just how much of an effective defence these sharp spines can be. They will then try digging around the immobilised hedgehog, circling all the while and getting absolutely nowhere. After a few more failed attempts at biting through those spines, the youngster will soon give up and move on elsewhere. However, if a vixen with young has learnt the knack of killing hedgehogs, she will then show her growing cubs how to do this. They simply watch and learn and then enjoy the reward for her labours. Like badgers, who quickly master this art, no doubt because 'brocks' will spend much time hunting together as a family group, the sow passing on her skills to the next generation, foxes need to learn how to turn the hedgehog over and kill it by biting the belly area and eating it thus. Hard terriers will often kill these largely harmless creatures by biting through the spines and crushing them, and Rock was terrible for this, but foxes and badgers will use other, more cunning, means. This is because they must avoid injury. If they receive an injury to the mouth, then starvation will usually result, if they do not recover quickly, so a fox, or a badger, will not risk such injuries by simply biting through the spines of hedgehogs, despite this being well within their capabilities. Big cats out in the wild, if they prey on porcupines, are at great risk of mouth injuries and some do get spines stuck in their gums. If they cannot quickly remove such spines, they go down hill fast and will usually die because of the injury.

Squirrels are another quarry species that foxes prey upon, though they are only successful at catching them when they mount a very patient stalk, waiting in the undergrowth until a squirrel is far enough away from a tree to have any chance of success. Squirrels can do great damage to many of our native trees and so foxes preying upon them, as well as other predators such as stoats and birds of prey, can only be a good thing. However, they are so difficult to catch, especially when they get among the branches of a tree, that this predation will be rather ineffective in controlling their numbers. True, stoats and, indeed, foxes, are excellent climbers, but they are no match for squirrels and have no chance at all of catching them in this environment. Squirrels will sometimes feed, or gather nuts, at quite large distances from trees at times and it is then that they become much more vulnerable. I have seen squirrels leaping massive distances as they jump into a neighbouring tree in order to get away from a predator.

Birds also make up a large part of the diet of foxes, though they are not easy to catch. But still, where foxes are found in large numbers, ground nesting birds will be few and far between, for foxes will raid nests during springtime and either eat eggs, or young, as well as any adult birds that can be caught. Woodpigeons make up quite a large part of the diet of a fox and Reynard will stalk them while they feed around the edges of woodland and pasture. I regularly find the remains of these birds while out walking and so they must feature prominently in their diet. Magpies and crows also fall victim, but far less frequently than do pigeons. Foxes are excellent climbers and so the nests of quite a few species of bird are raided by them. Some claim that foxes, as well as other predator species, will only prey on the sick and the weak. This is nonsense. Foxes are opportunistic hunters. They do not plan a night's hunting and then put that plan into operation. They simply foray and take the opportunities that come their way. True, they may kill a lot of sick, or injured prey, but that is simply because healthier stock is much sharper and gets away more readily.

It isn't just birds and small mammals that fall victim to the fox as it hunts for survival. Frogs, snails, beetles, earthworms and other insects are also eaten. In fact, at times such 'small-fry' makes up quite a large part of the diet and I have found scats that have contained almost nothing but beetle shells. Fruit is also enjoyed. Almost any kind of berry will be eaten by foxes and during the autumn, if one searches for scats, these droppings are a blackish purple in colour, due entirely to feeding on blackberries. Bilberries are also enjoyed. These grow profusely on heather moors and moorland foxes will feast on them during the later months of the year.

The vixen will begin to come into breeding condition during late December and dog foxes will then start wandering all over the place in search of a mate. The screams of foxes, an eerie sound, can be heard during the pitch-black winter nights around this time and dog foxes will travel great distances in answer to such calls. One can always tell a dog fox that has wandered in from another territory during this time of the year. If a dog fox is encountered by hounds, then he will make straight away back to his own country and some incredibly long hunts have occurred in these circumstances. Foxes that give such long runs, in the fells, are known as 'straight-necked', because of their making straightaway for home, despite this often being many miles away.

Mating and breeding

Mating will occur several times from late December through to early February, but only after the dog fox has fought off his rivals. Sometimes these are many, while at other times they may only have to fight off competition on only a couple of occasions. It all depends on the availability of vixens. If dog foxes are struggling to find a suitable mate in their own territory, they will then invade another and may win a mate from the dominant dog fox of that area, or be thrashed and sent packing! Injuries can occur during these fights, but few are so serious as to threaten survival, for once dominance has been established, the fight will cease, due to the submissive member turning and fleeing. Foxes mate in exactly the same way as dogs, becoming tied for a period of time. Mating will usually take place out in the open, though, where earths are large enough, such as under old mill ruins where cellars and old, now unused, water tunnels give plenty of room, mating may occur underground. Foxes are certainly vulnerable at these times, but few will be encountered by the hunter of foxes. Mating will very often occur during the early morning, or late evening, when hounds are not hunting, so it is the shooter of foxes, those who stalk during the early morning, or late evening, who are most likely to see this occurrence.

Just over seven weeks later, the vixen will give birth inside an earth she has chosen for herself and the type of earth chosen differs greatly, depending on the type of country they inhabit. Fell foxes, for instance, will usually choose a rock lair for rearing cubs, while in the shires the chosen den is very often either a dug-out rabbit hole, or an old abandoned badger sett. The vixen will not allow the dog fox near her while giving birth and she will not tolerate him having contact with her cubs for at least the first few days, though dog foxes will not have much to do with them until weaning occurs.

Sometimes a vixen from the previous year's litter will remain with her mother and help with the rearing of the new family, but this does not always happen. It is the dog fox who is the main provider of food for the vixen for the first couple of weeks. After that, she will hunt and catch much of her own food, though she will not spend too much time away from her youngsters.

The cubs are born blind, but with a good covering of fur, for the den floor will be simply bare rock or earth, with few, if any, comforts. If left for long periods during the first couple of weeks or so, they would be in grave danger of dying from the cold, for fox earths are not the warmest of places. True, they are deep enough not to allow the frost to penetrate, but still, they are not in any way warm. That is, not until the vixen lies below with her family. She will rear them inside a small chamber and her body heat acts much in the same way as central heating. The cubs will be warmed by her, but at the same time the chamber warms up until it can be almost tropical inside a fox den. As the cubs grow, they will keep each other warm and, to a certain extent, the chamber too. Also, a barren vixen from a previous litter will often remain with her mother and help rear the young family of foxes and she too will help to keep the inner chamber warm and cosy for the babies, something that is essential during those first few days of their new lives.

A vixen will care diligently for her youngsters and, alongside the dog fox, will hunt prey throughout the night and very often during daylight hours too. Foxes are not exactly clean creatures and so earths will soon become stinking with rotting carcasses. When things get too bad, the vixen will often move her cubs to another den, for disease may strike where conditions are particularly filthy. Also, if there are any disturbances close to the breeding earth, or human scent is detected nearby, or around the den, the vixen will move her cubs straight away, even while it is light, if she feels they are in imminent danger. This, again, demonstrates both the cunning of foxes and their diligent care for their growing family.

Quite a few years ago a local shepherd was suffering serious troubles from foxes preying on his lambs. Over thirty had been taken and as a result he had moved many of his flock into his barn for protection, while Tim and I dealt with the troubles. Tim had gone on his own one Sunday morning and had thoroughly searched the place with his lurcher; a son of Brian Plummer's famous Merle. This lurcher, like his sire, was an extremely good fox dog and he marked a large rockpile on the edge of a quarry, which borders this land we were hunting. Tim immediately headed for my house and asked if I would bring the terriers along and deal with the culprits. Rock and Bella, her daughter, were coupled and taken to the spot and sure enough there were many signs of cubs all around the place, with stinking remains of all kinds of prey, including lambs, scattered about. Rock was put in and the very fact that she entered was a sure sign that the rock earth was full of fox scent. However, her prompt return quickly informed us that the vixen had moved them in the short space of time it had taken Tim to fetch me. That vixen's diligent care and cunning had saved her family.

We later found where she had moved them to. They were in an old abandoned quarry and we found seven lamb carcasses scattered about those huge rocks. The earth was utterly undiggable and massive in area, but still, we put in the terriers in the hopes that they would deal with the cubs inside and it wasn't long before Rock and Bella were baying like fiends and scratching at the unyielding rocks in their frustration. The cubs got themselves into very tight spots and there was absolutely no way they could reach them. Tim and I spent hours attempting to open up a way through for them, as we dug in likely places, but our efforts were in vain and made little impact anyway, so we were forced to give them best. We later dug a small vixen from this spot, which had chosen a rather shallow part of this rockpile to shelter in, and shot two other foxes, at last stopping the predation for another year, but still, the shepherd had lost a large part of his livelihood before we had been able to put a stop to their antics.

At another place, a dairy farm where poultry was also kept, the farmer's sons found a dug-out rabbit hole with plenty of signs of cubs all around, which they had searched for after losing stock. They called in Roy and myself to deal with them, but by the time we got there the vixen had already begun shifting her family else-where. However, we were a little too quick for her. The terriers, Rock and Pep, marked eagerly, so there was at least one cub still inside that lair. Of course, at the time, we knew nothing of the vixen's cunning plan, but it soon became apparent as the evening's events unfolded. It was a lovely sunny spring evening and Roy and

I arrived at the farm after a hard day at work. The earth was a two-holer and Pep marked one end, while Rock marked the other. The place was extremely tight and the two terriers began digging into the tunnel and slowly making their way towards each other, with the cubs somewhere about the middle, we thought.

A dense woodland stands at the bottom of this large pasture and as we began digging a fox stood barking just under the cover of trees, maybe a hundred yards away. It was obvious then that the vixen had already started shifting her family, sensing they were in danger. She was obviously barking to a cub, or cubs, still remaining inside and so we pressed on, hoping to account for at least one fox for the farmer. This was late spring and the cubs were undoubtedly well grown by this time, so the farmer insisted they be dealt with. But as we were digging, Pep emerged from the hole she was attempting to get through, intent on finding another way in to her quarry. We hadn't bothered blocking any of the tunnels, for the terriers themselves prevented a bolt from being possible, or so we thought. As she did so, a large cub bolted and ran off down the field, disappearing into the wood and being led away by the vixen and dog fox, which had joined its mate in barking to the cub. The terriers soon told that the earth was now vacant and so we stopped the dig and headed off in search of the new earth instead, the farmer more than a little irritated at the great escape we had just witnessed; another display of great cunning and determination to survive, as well as the tender care of both parents for their youngsters. Despite our best efforts and a large-scale search, we never did find those cubs. She undoubtedly moved them well away from the farm and her efforts succeeded in saving herself and her family.

Such efforts are not always successful, however. A vixen once moved cubs into a large rockpile, which bordered a farm where the occupier hated the vulpine race with a passion, after losing large numbers of his livestock to foxes over many years. She had obviously been disturbed by something, either the risk of disease, or discovery at the previous lair, and had moved her family to what she considered a much safer haven. I found the remains of chickens, taken from the nearby farm, at the rockpile and my bitch quickly entered. Soon afterwards, the vixen bolted from a part of the rockpile where covering it with a lurcher was impossible, so she succeeded in getting away, but not so her cubs. Rock finished them all below ground and returned soon after with one of them. It was well grown and old enough for the vixen to abandon it to its fate. Rock's lack of interest thereafter confirmed that no live foxes were skulking below ground. The chicken losses stopped and the farmer could relax once more. I hate hunting foxes during the springtime, but one has no choice but to do so when a farmer is suffering from such losses to his livestock.

Derek Webster was recently called to a keepered spot after a fox had been seen in a certain area of the estate. Derek and Paul Stead travelled down to this spot, a place Derek has hunted for many years, and checked out likely earths. They found the breeding earth shortly afterwards, but Rocky, Derek's lurcher, and Paul's terriers, showed little interest. The vixen had either got wind of their discovery, probably because of human scent nearby, or the earth was so full of stinking carcasses that she deemed it necessary to move the youngsters. However, she chose a very insecure place to hide them, probably mid-way between the move, and the terriers and lurcher quickly accounted for seven cubs. A vixen will usually give birth to four or five in a litter, but as many as seven can be born, especially when food supplies are abundant, such as on a keepered estate. The gamekeeper was just about to put young pheasants out, so you can imagine how grateful he was that Derek and Paul had caught up with this family of foxes that would undoubtedly have taken many of the young stock.

The cubs, up until around the fifth week, are of a chocolate brown in colour, which gradually fades to the usual russet-red. Their eyes begin to open at around ten to fourteen days of age and that is when they will begin getting around the den a little better, though, until four or five weeks of age, they will mainly remain in the birth chamber. They will be fully weaned by the age of six weeks, though they may have taken regurgitated food from as early as three weeks, depending on the availability of milk from their mother. If a vixen has an abundant milk supply, then the cubs will not be weaned until they reach four weeks of age. When they begin eating more solid food, the vixen will help them along by tearing open the flesh so that the cubs can more easily access their meals. Once they reach the age of around two months, the parents will begin bringing injured prey for them to kill.

Fox watching at this time of the year is most exciting and very rewarding. The watcher will enjoy sights of adult foxes, as well as of cubs, and they will witness much play between the individuals making up a litter. This play activity is simply a rehearsal for adult life and many skills learned in play will actually mean their survival when they begin life on their own. Also, these 'toy fights' teach skills that will enable dog foxes to make a stand both for territory, and for a vixen. The art of submission is also learnt. Foxes do not fight to the death. When superiority has been established, the defeated combatant will submit and slink away. The more dominant in play will soon have the others submitting and yet another important lesson is learned. If foxes did not learn to submit to the more dominant among them, then fights to the death, or serious injury, would occur. And foxes must at all costs avoid serious injury, for an injured fox cannot catch prey and so will die. Some try to survive by raiding chicken houses, or killing lambs, when injured, but this usually ends in death too, for a farmer will call in hounds, lurchers, terriers, or the gun, in order to have the culprit dealt with. And injured foxes are not difficult to catch up with.

Young foxes will stay with their mother for the best part of the summer, even into autumn, though some young dog foxes will have left the family before summer is out. A young vixen may stay with her mother and help rear cubs during the following spring, though this does not always occur. The majority of fox families I have watched have consisted of dog, vixen and cubs. In some cases, more than one barren vixen will help with rearing a litter. This, in some ways, is a good thing. During springtime the fox family, generally, is left to get on with their business without disturbance, unless, that is, they choose a keepered estate as their home, or begin raiding hen houses, or fields full of lambs. It is then that the hunting of foxes continues, when, usually, the off-season is being observed.

Before the hunting ban in England, Wales and Scotland, a very effective system could be employed that would mean the guilty fox, that is, the one taking farm livestock, would very often be dealt with, while others that were not troublesome were left to carry on with their affairs without hindrance. The hunting ban now means that such measures cannot be employed and this can only be a bad thing for the fox population. However, more of this in another chapter. Whatever means employed, the need for control when livestock is being taken will inevitably result, in many cases, in either the dog fox, or, worse still, the vixen being killed. This, on the surface, spells disaster for a litter of cubs. However, that is not always necessarily the case.

First of all, unless the actual breeding den is discovered early on, which is unlikely as there is little activity going on there until the cubs are weaned and begin venturing outside, the vixen gives off little scent while pregnant and while the cubs are very young. This means that hunting dogs will not be able to stick to the line of a vixen and so the chances of the discovery of the earth during the first few weeks of the cubs' lives are very slim indeed. If a vixen is killed once the cubs are weaned, then survival for them is almost assured, especially if a barren vixen has been helping rear the youngsters. True, many vixens are killed while rearing cubs, because of their antics with farm livestock, or young pheasant poults, but their youngsters often go on to reach maturity. Sometimes though, if a keeper shoots a vixen and she is obviously rearing a litter, he will look for the den and finish the cubs too.

Foxes though, will sometimes choose an earth that is impossible to dig and very often actually accounting for the cubs, proves difficult indeed. When a terrier is entered the cubs will very often head off into extremely tight places where a terrier just cannot get. This is especially true of rock earths. I was once hunting an old quarry and my Jack Russell terrier entered an earth inside a massive pile of old tyres at the foot of a sheer rock face. The remains of chickens etc, soon betrayed the fact that cubs were at home, but they managed to get themselves into incredibly tight spots out of reach of the terrier and so they had to be left for another day.

Despite being hunted relentlessly, the fox population has boomed over recent decades and this has much to do with the fact that busy roads and built-up areas have put a stop to many places being hunted with hounds, or, indeed, terriers and lurchers. Hunting saved the severely decimated fox population in the first place and allowed numbers to increase until a healthy population became established, particularly during the twentieth century, and such hunting maintained that population, but in non-hunted

61

areas the population has got out of hand, resulting in very poor specimens which spread mange and other diseases. Despite these facts though, which fully support the hunting of foxes, much opposition to what some folk see as 'cruelty', has resulted in a ban, not on actually killing foxes, but on following dogs which hunt them. Can the killing of foxes be justified in the first place?

CHAPTER THREE

WHY CONTROL FOX NUMBERS?

FOXES are incredibly beautiful creatures and the sight of one crossing fields, or wandering through woodland, or, better still, across mountain and moorland, is a thrilling scene indeed. Their colour and dense fur make them most attractive and the thought of such creatures being hunted, by whatever means, is incredibly repellent to many folk. Although I believe that many have campaigned against hunting out of sheer class hatred, rather than concern for the welfare of animals, I also believe that many act out of sincerity and I am sure they truly believe that there is absolutely no justification whatsoever, for the hunting of such a lovely creature. In view of this, we should ask ourselves if foxes should be hunted at all. Can we really justify the killing of this beautiful animal?

When chef Antony Worral Thompson was asked by Anne Robinson if he agreed with hunting, during the 'Test The Nation' quiz, he answered that he did, then went on to give his reason for this. Sixty-two of his chickens had been killed by just one fox and this was the reason he agreed with the hunting of foxes. And this sort of statement is repeated throughout the country. Admittedly, sixty-two chickens is an extremely high number to lose, but a dozen or more can easily be lost in just one raid and many people are baffled by the behaviour of foxes when they get in among large numbers of fowl and slaughter them as if they were trying to satisfy an insatiable bloodlust. This sort of behaviour, however, can easily be explained.

The fox is out on the prowl and the drifting scent of chickens is captured on the breeze, leading him to a hen house that remains open, or the door hasn't been secured properly, or maybe it is slightly rotten and the fox digs and chews his way through it in a

63

matter of seconds, rather than minutes. The hens begin clucking nervously as the fox breaks through the barrier and finally enters the dark interior. And then, all of a sudden, he is in among a flapping horde of birds in sheer panic. He strikes, strikes again, and again, and again. Before he knows it, several birds lie dead, flapping around no more. The same can happen with ducks too. An allotment holder who is a friend of Tim, my one-time hunting partner, lost sixteen ducks one night, when a fox got in among them, with only one actually being taken. What a waste this is. But why do foxes behave in such a seemingly wasteful manner?

The first reason for this is simply because the fox is an opportunistic hunter which takes chances at catching prey as they arise. Experience will dictate which hunts are most likely to succeed and which are best left, and a hen house full to bursting with succulent prey will be irresistible to a fox. The opportunity to kill presents itself, even tenfold, and so Reynard takes his chance and slaughters the unfortunate creatures around him, which have nowhere to run to. He is simply taking the opportunity that has arisen. Secondly, predators such as foxes have a strong instinct to cache, that is, to bury food for times that prove much leaner, when prey is difficult to come across. And so when a fox kills several chickens, or ducks, or, indeed, lambs, it is simply obeying its instinct to kill during times of plenty, in readiness for times of virtually nothing. True, a fox will take only one chicken and will not return immediately in order to bury, or cache, the surplus, either because it simply forgets about the rest, or the taint of man in the area puts it off, now that the hunger pangs have been satisfied. When hunger strikes again, however, then the fox may return, possibly looking for the surplus, but finding only live hens and, if the stock is not properly secured, having a go at these instead. So to call foxes cruel, vicious, evil, as though they kill just for sheer pleasure, is totally unfounded.

When a fox kills in this manner it is simply following an age-old instinct of survival. Nevertheless, such actions can cause utter devastation on a farm and livelihoods can be seriously threatened. Especially when organic chicken farming is practised, are the hens at risk, though chickens farmed in any way, on whatever scale, are at risk. True, if a structure is sound and the hens are locked up at night, then they should be safe, but actually getting the hens in at night is not always possible. I know of a doctor who bought a house out in the country and began keeping a few chickens in order to enjoy fresh eggs for his family. Foxes wiped them out in no time at all and after restocking they did so again. Foxes will sometimes strike during daylight hours, so locking them up at night is not the perfect solution it at first seems to be. Foxes can chew and dig through wood that isn't too thick, whether it be rotten or otherwise, and so, again, locking them up is not always effective. At the Holcombe Hunt kennels, hens are kept and they run loose about the place, being locked up at night, but still, many have been lost to foxes and, at one time, the Huntsman almost gave up keeping them, he lost that many, despite a kennel full of hounds being only yards away!

This predation on hens, when a fox will take them either by raiding the hen house at night, or by raiding the stock during daylight hours, which is a common occurrence, and killing up to a dozen and more, while taking just the one, is one reason why the hunting of foxes is fully justified. Do not forget, foxes are in the business of survival and a farmyard full of fat hens is going to be a place of plenty and that means that several visits will occur and several more hens will be lost. Vixens will teach their cubs throughout the summer months, leading them on nightly jaunts in search of prey and teaching them much in preparation of them leaving the 'nest' during the autumn. If she has successfully preyed upon farm livestock such as hens, then she will teach such methods to her cubs. Hence the reason for fox control. With this in mind, one can understand why, during earlier centuries, when a fox raided livestock, the whole village would turn out in order to hunt it down and put a stop to its crimes. The fox would simply be surviving, not waging a personal vendetta against humankind, but still, when livelihoods are threatened, that fox must be dealt with.

It is not just hens and ducks that fall victim to foxes, however. The same can be said for geese, lambs and piglets. Sometimes scores of piglets are taken by foxes, particularly vixens rearing cubs, and they can be a real nuisance in areas where pig farming is practised on a large scale. Thirsk, in North Yorkshire, the home, in fact, of the veterinary practice of James Herriot and Siegfried Farnon (Alf Wight and Donald Sinclair), is an area where pig farming is traditionally practised and Frank Buck and Cyril Breay, the creators of what are now known as Patterdale terriers (see *The*

Patterdale Terrier, Seán Frain, published by Swan Hill Press) would often hunt down foxes that were preying on piglets at farms in this area. Max Buck, Frank's son, also shifts foxes for pig farmers in this area, as they can cause much damage. He dug a fox at an earth close to a pig farm that was littered with their carcasses, many of them untouched. Again, the vixen was simply acting on instinct, killing plenty in times of plenty, but, again, this cannot be allowed to continue and fully justifies the need for controlling fox numbers.

I have seen the suffering fox predation can cause among the farming community. I have seen shepherds bringing their flocks into farm outbuildings not suited to such uses, out of sheer desperation because they were losing so many lambs. Again, foxes can kill far more than they eat in this situation. I have seen lambs left for dead, with holes through their skulls where the fox has attacked them, but not finished them off before moving onto the next. Most lambs in this situation have to be put down, for many are brain damaged. Some recover, but very few. Others have their heads bitten off and the body is just left lying on the ground, while others are left whole, killed by a bite through the throat, or skull. Again, a fox is simply acting on instinct and is taking prey that cannot be very effectively defended by the ewe, but such losses cannot go unpunished and a lamb-killing fox must be stopped. True, not all foxes will kill lambs. Some just do not have the stomach for facing an angry ewe intent on defending her youngster, especially when easier prey can be had, but those foxes that do take to this form of hunting cannot be allowed to carry on. A shepherd I have hunted foxes for, for many years, lost several lambs during one spring and a ewe had half of her hind leg eaten away by a fox, while struggling to give birth to her lamb. The culprit was coming out of a nearby quarry where they couldn't be got at, but lamping at night with a gun soon stopped the predation.

Lambing troubles very often end by around the middle of May, when the lambs have grown bigger, but some foxes will continue to prey on them even into the autumn. I once found a large late August lamb that had been killed by a fox. Dogs generally tear when killing lambs, but this one had been cleanly killed with a bite to the throat and the holes where the fangs had pierced through were clearly visible. Also, this was right out on the moors where

Controlling foxes is essential in sheep-rearing country – foxes prey on lambs.

dogs, generally speaking, just do not roam. So foxes can, and do, take larger lambs. This desire to prey on a shepherd's flock is just one more reason why fox numbers must be controlled. The fact that several can be lost to foxes in just one night lends some urgency to the need for control.

When in among chickens, or, indeed, ducks and geese, the noise from the panic-stricken birds very often alerts the farmer and the fox will usually high-tail it out of there rather rapidly, leaving carnage in its wake. A score and more can be lost in this situation and the sight of dead birds all over the place is devastating to someone who strives to make a living from livestock. Where a fox is not disturbed whilst in among fowl, some of the carcasses may be found half-buried. Again, as mentioned earlier, this is because of the desire to cache food during times of plenty and this attempt to bury reserves for later, lends weight to my theory that killing several birds at just one visit is sparked by this instinct to store food for leaner times. Foxes do not act out of bloodlust, or cruelty, but seen from a human standpoint, this act certainly seems cruel and totally unjustified.

During the springtime, large country estates, as well as small rough shoots, will put down pheasants and possibly partridge for when the shooting season begins again in the autumn and these fresh stocks provide a massive amount of food supplies for local

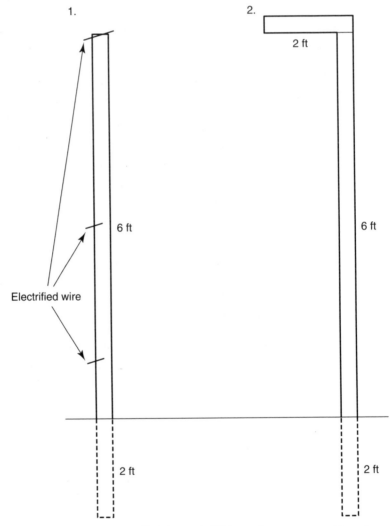

1.

2.

2 ft

6 ft   6 ft

Electrified wire

2 ft   2 ft

Fox proof fencing. 1. Electrified fence. 2. With overhang to prevent jumping over. Height and ground depth are the minimum. Strong mesh is necessary.

fox populations. And where food is plentiful, foxes will have larger litters of six or even seven cubs. Litters larger than this are usually the result of two vixens birthing in the same earth and this occurrence is really quite common. It was once thought that such things only occurred on moorland and fell, but even in the shires large litters have been found that could only belong to two, or even three, vixens.

Not only will foxes prey upon adult pheasants, but youngsters, known as poults, will also fall victim and if a fox gets in among young pheasants, then carnage will usually result. That same instinct kicks in and several will be slaughtered during one brief visit. And so fox control is very strictly carried out on keepered estates. A country estate in the north of England, where Derek Webster has been assisting with fox control for many years, once employed a head gamekeeper who was rather slack when it came to controlling their numbers. Foxes were found in abundance on this place and they fed well from the large stock of pheasants put down each springtime. The winter corn and food put out for pheasants also meant a large rat population could help support the fox numbers and litters must have been large. Also, small rodents were killed and eaten by these foxes and so birds of prey such as owls, were few and far between. Hares were almost non-existent.

When the new keeper took over he immediately implemented a fox control programme and set about drastically reducing their numbers using terriers, lurchers and the gun. Foxes were dug with the terriers, or bolted to waiting lurchers, or the gun, and they were lamped at night, using the gun in the main, with lurchers being used on occasion. I have been with Derek controlling both rats and foxes on this estate and the keeper told me of how he had large piles of dead foxes in the yard in those days, there were so many of them. Nowadays, foxes are only found in small numbers, just the odd one or two, and so the balance of the estate has returned. Visiting this place is like stepping into a paradise for wildlife. Obviously, pheasant and partridge thrive here now, when once their numbers were largely depleted due to supporting a large number of foxes. Small bird populations thrive also, with few predators to threaten them. Small rodents are found in abundance and there are owl-nesting boxes all over the estate. Foxes no longer drastically reduce the numbers of these rodents and so they support a large owl population, as well as other birds of prey such as kestrels, which are no threat whatsoever to game stocks. Also, the hares have recovered dramatically and five and six can be put up in just one field. The place is thriving with wildlife now, but only since fox numbers were drastically reduced, which tells us much about whether or not fox control is necessary. I have witnessed this oasis for wildlife myself and am fully convinced that control benefits not only our farmers but also our wildlife. True, foxes have a right to exist, but not in such high numbers so as to affect wildlife populations such as ground-nesting birds and hares. Control is not, and never should be, about elimination, just maintaining a healthy number of foxes that do not decimate any other species of wildlife, or domestic live-stock.

Derek was called in during one spring, to check out if any foxes had chosen the estate for breeding purposes. Country estates are very attractive places for vixens to rear cubs, due entirely to the large pheasant and partridge populations, as well as wildlife such as small birds and hares, and so a diligent keeper always takes care to keep an eye out for foxes taking his stock in order to support a

Derek Webster's Rocky – an excellent fox-catching lurcher.

large, growing family. Derek and a couple of friends walked round parts of the estate and at one spot, by a brook, the terrier, a Border, marked keenly. A collar was fitted and the keeper stationed himself in a likely spot with his gun, just in case Reynard bolted. The Border, a keen fox dog, entered and soon after began baying loudly. The terrier was given time to bolt its quarry, but it had settled in one place from the outset and so the owner began sweeping the ground with the locator box, in search of that elusive bleeping that would signal the start of a dig.

Sure enough, the locator sounded its call soon afterwards and the dial turned down until a reading of five foot was displayed, which isn't too deep, especially in soft soil such as is found on this estate. A square of turf was cut out and digging operations began in earnest, while the Border terrier continued at its fox with great eagerness indeed. At about four feet down, another reading was taken and the dial was almost at the 'off' mark, signalling that they were right on top of the terrier by this time. A little more digging, going cautiously and carefully now, and at last the soil crumbled and the hole opened up. After clearing a space around the terrier, the owner then pulled it out, expecting to be facing a rather belligerent fox, the terrier had made that much noise, but instead he was greeted by the sight of a shelduck sitting on eggs, which then got up off the nest, waddled out of the hole and promptly plopped into the water, before casually swimming away and leaving an embarrassed bunch of hunters in its wake!

Although this was a lot of hard work for nothing, it pales into insignificance when compared with someone I know who dug much deeper to his terrier, only to end up embarrassed and ashamed. This chap was notorious for creating false marking terriers because of his habit of getting his terriers all fired up at whichever earth they came to, whether it be occupied or otherwise. I had fallen victim to one of his false marking terriers in the past. A Patterdale terrier I was hunting with, but did not own I am glad to say, had bayed at a rock while I and a couple of other lads had dug to him, through difficult stone and rock-filled soil. But now the tables were turned. This chap got his hands on a Jack Russell terrier, which was a little corker at fox. On a visit to Cheshire, the terrier was put to ground and he began baying deep inside the lair, only just being audible. A mark, after allowing time for the terrier to settle, was gained on the locator and it read eight feet. Digging began and the going was hard. Eight feet is quite some distance to be digging into the earth and tons of soil were taken out of the ever-deepening trench. Some time later, they broke through to the terrier and discovered that it was baying at a rabbit! One can imagine how blue the air turned that day.

This, of course, was not the fault of the terrier. He had a very distinguished career behind him and he had served with a few hunts, as well as having worked privately, acquitting himself very well indeed. He had just fallen into the wrong hands. On discovering that going into earths and baying, even if it was at rabbits, was pleasing to his master and he was rewarded for it, it became natural for him to do this. Thankfully, after being written off as 'useless' by the more than useless new keeper, the terrier was returned to its original owner, at one time a very good terrierman, and he soon had the terrier living up to its former glory once more. In Staffordshire, where this terrierman had permission on a massive country estate, his lurcher flushed a fox out of the winter crops put down for pheasant feed and cover, and chased it across the field. Feeling the hot breath of the dog on its flank, Reynard chose to seek sanctuary below ground and fled to a spot under a hedge – a dug-out rabbit burrow consisting of three holes. Of course, the terrier was put in and soon began baying, with digging operations commencing soon after.

The terrier, as is the norm, was given a little time to settle, and to see if the fox would bolt, but Reynard was having none of it. The lurcher had pursued it relentlessly and the fox was not for facing that treatment again, choosing to stay below instead. The digging, however, was incredibly difficult, as anyone who has attempted digging under a hedge will understand. Not only is the digger greatly hampered by the hedge itself, which cannot be dug up and moved out of the way, but one has to dig through and around large tangles of roots which make the going incredibly arduous. However, a determined terrierman, if it is at all possible, will usually get there in the end and, sure enough the terrier was reached three hours later. He had latched onto his fox and was attempting to draw it out. The fox was accounted for and the terrier vindicated, the previous owner shown up as a complete idiot when it came to terriers and their work. Scores of terriers are written off as 'useless' when, very often, the fault lies with the owner. Wrong entering methods are very often to blame, though sometimes, as in this case, a good experienced terrier can be almost ruined when in the wrong hands.

Because of the habits of foxes when preying upon farm livestock and game birds, as well as wildlife such as ground-nesters, he is hunted relentlessly and, as we have seen, rightly so. But that does not mean that the controlling of fox numbers is an easy business. Foxes, as discussed in an earlier chapter, are incredibly cunning and this wily nature is often displayed in the types of earth Reynard will choose to lie-up in. One of his best tricks is to get himself into a dense tangle of tree roots from where he can usually dominate the situation. Ghyll was in his early years working foxes and on this occasion I was out hunting with just him.

I was checking out a hill farm and I headed for the earth below a tree on Peewit hill. Foxes had dug into a long established rabbit burrow a couple of years earlier, undoubtedly in order to secure their prey, but I had never actually found any inside this two-holer. Ghyll was a game terrier who eventually learned how to finish foxes without taking too much punishment, but this was during his early entering, so he had not yet figured out how best to deal with his quarry. Still, he was making great progress and I was hoping to further his entering on this occasion by enjoying a decent dig, if I could find a fox at home. Sure enough, Ghyll was keen when I tried him at the entrance and so I loosed him and he disappeared below ground immediately. He began baying a short time afterwards and I gave him a little time to settle, before heading to the nearby farm for digging tackle. Trevor was pleased that I had a fox to ground, for he was not at all keen on them, coming from a long line of Lancashire sheep farmers, and he gladly loaned me the necessary tools.

On returning to the earth, Ghyll was still baying strong and steady and the mark on the locator was easily picked up. His quarry wasn't deep, at around three feet or so, but as I began chopping into the frosty turf, I realised that this was going to be no easy dig, for a thin covering of grass and soil soon gave way to heavy clay. The morning was crisp and a ground frost lay heavily on the broad sweeping pastures all around, a cold northerly breeze blowing, yet I was soon sweating and down to just a T-shirt in no time at all, the loud, thunderous bay of my terrier at his work, spurring me on. I could hear Ghyll dodging out of the way every time the irritated fox lunged at him, striking with surprising speed, the bangs and bumps signalling that he had come into contact with the walls of the tunnel as he 'bobbed and weaved'. He carried on undaunted, however, in true working terrier fashion, revelling in the contest being waged in the pitch-blackness below.

I attempted to dig down from above and the going was never easy, but it soon became apparent that going any further was just about impossible. I knew I had struck thick, impenetrable tree roots when the spade bounced back at me after ramming it violently into the clay. I attempted to dig around them, but they were everywhere and successfully barred my way down to the fox, which had obviously dug into them in order to give itself maximum protection. Having realised I was wasting my time attempting to go any further, I quickly back-filled and replaced the turf, before beginning to dig into the hillside below the tree. Again, heavy clay needed to be cut through and a few large stones were in my way as I dug in, with much greater difficulty than digging down from the top.

This was an awkward spot and I was forced to dig while on my knees, which takes away some of the power one can put into digging when in an upright position. But at least I was making progress, even if it was slow. Had this been a 'normal' earth, just a dug-out rabbit hole in soil (which, when compared to rock earths, are few and far between in these Pennine districts), I would have been down to my fox within half an hour, but as it was I was still cutting into that hillside three hours later, my terrier still going at his fox, despite the difficulties and his inexperience. I thrust the spade in and the familiar dull thud, as well as the spade bouncing back and jarring my hands and wrists badly, told the familiar story of roots in my way yet again. This time, though, I found a way through, but it grew narrower and narrower as I continued on, digging out an ever-deepening tunnel into that hillside. But it was no good. Only inches from the fox, the way proved impossible and there were no other angles I could try. I was beaten. Reluctantly, I eventually managed to call Ghyll back after his hard stint to ground, back-filled and then returned to the farm. Trevor just shrugged his shoulders, knowing full well that foxes cannot always be accounted for, and I returned home with my terrier. He had shown great promise that day, but still, I was not happy that he had not got to taste the carcass of his foe. That cunning fox had chosen an incredibly safe haven and had secured its brush as a result.

On another occasion, although tree roots gave sanctuary to a fox, we were more successful in the end, due to team effort and more than a little grit and determination. I was drawing a wood for rabbits, bushing them with my team of four terriers, when I saw Fell heading off into an adjacent wood. There are a couple of earths in this woodland and he had obviously set his mind on checking them out. When he didn't return, I knew that one of those earths must be occupied. And, sure enough, I soon found him baying loudly at a fox, which had got itself into a strong position in among the roots of a large, ancient tree. I had had a terrier to a fox for three and a half hours in this same place on an earlier visit, but that fox could not be shifted. However, I decided to still have a go, for Fell, as usual, was working his fox hard and there was no way of calling him out of there. So, again, I allowed him to settle and then walked the hundred yards to the farm where digging tackle was obtained.

This fox was in an incredibly tight spot and there was no way Fell could get around it in order to go for the throat hold which would have seen a successful conclusion to the whole affair. A fox will just strike from around the roots in this situation and it is difficult for a terrier to do anything else, but bay, nip and tease, until an opportunity presents itself, or the digger breaks through. Some terriers, of course, will go jaw to jaw in these circumstances, but the damage inflicted on a terrier in this situation can be pretty horrific. Fell, thankfully, teased and bayed at his fox cleverly and the digging began while he did so. I had not fitted a locator collar, for I was only rabbiting, but that didn't matter, for he was only two or three feet deep and easily audible as he bayed at his foe eagerly.

There was only one hole to this earth and it led right under the base of the tree. I began digging on the opposite side, as close to the tree as I possibly could, and found the going difficult indeed. There were stones, some large, others small, which made things far from easy, and then, just a few inches down, I hit clay. This earth is only a couple of fields away from Peewit hill, so the whole area must be grounded on clay. The clay was hard enough, but to make things worse, it wasn't long before I began hitting roots, though, thankfully, none of them were too thick and so, after a lot of effort and a bucket or two full of sweat, I managed to cut through them and shift them out of the way. Fell was getting louder and louder and I was now only inches from him. It was then that I began hitting the massively thick roots that were part of the mainstay of this grand tree. However, with some effort, I managed to clear a way around them and soon broke through.

I made the hole as big as I possibly could, but still I was working in a very tight opening and Fell was about four inches into the hole, his head lunging in and out of the roots as he worked his foe hard. I was nearer to the fox, at this point, than I was to my terrier, though I couldn't quite see it because of a large root that shielded it from view, as well as from Fell's efforts to shift it from this vantage point. Also, the terrier was having to work uphill, which made things worse for him. Despite this, however, he continued on undaunted, determined to win the day.

Turk was in his early days of entering at this time and he was showing great promise. He is sired by Fell and Mist is his dam, both of which were very experienced at fox before I bred from them. Turk had bushed a number of foxes by this time, but he had begun working earths too. We were out a few weeks before this dig and the terriers were busily bushing rabbits around a spinney on the edge of an old quarry. Turk picked a scent up and disappeared into a rockpile that normally holds a decent number of rabbits. I have ferreted this rockpile many times and bolted several rabbits over the years, but foxes have been conspicuous by their absence. However, on this occasion a fox was at home and Turk was quickly onto it, bolting it and coming out almost on its brush. He then chased it across the heather and rock and the rest of the terriers joined him, hunting it across the quarry until they finally lost it as the warm sunshine of early autumn rapidly eliminated all traces of scent.

Turk was keen to go at this hole and so I loosed him and tried him at the spot I had opened up. He entered the tight spot carefully and managed to get his head and shoulders around the large root, grabbing his quarry and slowly drawing it out from its sanctuary. Turk is a large terrier of fourteen, maybe fifteen, inches and he is a powerful dog. Despite the efforts of his foe, he was able to draw it out and the quarry was secured. Fell was in an impossible situation, working uphill in a tight place, with a fox continually striking from the safety of tree roots. Turk, however, came from a completely different angle and was working downhill and coming at his foe from the side. Also, he is a much more powerful dog than either his sire or dam, and so he was able to draw his quarry from out of that former safe haven. If I had not broke through where I did, I would never have succeeded on that day and the fox would have secured its brush.

Foxes, in the main, will choose earths that offer at least some protection, should they be disturbed. On some occasions, though, they pick places that are so easy to penetrate that it is hard to believe how daft they can sometimes be. Yes, they are cunning creatures for sure, but occasionally they leave themselves open to easy capture. One of the easiest places I have ever dug was a one-holer on a bracken-clad hillside below a long line of crags, known as High crags.

Crag, an unregistered Lakeland terrier, shot to ground and I knew then that something was at home, though rabbits are some-times found here and just for a minute I wondered if it was a bunny, rather than a fox, that he had found. However, the strong steady bay soon dispelled any such notions. Crag was a wonderful terrier for digging to. He was not hard and always worked sensibly, but he knew how to 'boss' his quarry and had proved most useful in a variety of earths. He was Middleton bred and, indeed, I had bought him from Gary, but he also had a dash of Ward blood in his veins. I had enjoyed a successful summer of shows with this terrier, which was typey and had a wonderfully hard jacket that kept all weathers at bay, no matter how severe, but this was now the middle of winter and showing was just a distant memory, now that work was of primary importance.

I usually go to the farm for digging tackle when such opportuni-ties arise, but a couple of friends accompanied me that day and so we had a stout spade and a hatchet with us. The locator collar was still in my pocket, for the earths under these crags are very shallow and such tools are not necessary. It took about five seconds to locate the spot where Crag was hard at work and, once the exit had been blocked by Jim, digging commenced. The moorland grasses are tough to get through, but still, it wasn't long before a neat square of turf was cut and pulled out. The soil underneath was very dry and full of roots, so the hatchet came in very handy for breaking this up. It was then very easy to remove the loosened soil with the spade. As we got deeper and ever-nearer to our quarry, the soil became much softer and thus easier to work with, now that we had surpassed the depths of those tangles of grass roots.

The barking, banging and bumping, was now very loud and so I began to go carefully as I cut into the final few inches before, at last, the ground suddenly gave and we were through, right on top of the terrier. All that was left to do was to clear a space around him that would give us room for manoeuvre. As I did so, Crag suddenly rushed in and seized his quarry by the cheek, so that it was unable to bite him. He hung on grimly and his prize was secured. This had been one of the easiest digs I had ever taken part in and one wonders why foxes will choose such places for their residence during daylight hours. Bolting foxes from such one-hole earths is difficult, for very often the fox cannot get past the terrier, but digging them out is child's play, even without a locator.

I have enjoyed quite a number of such digs, but usually, especially up here among the vast open spaces of the Pennines, the earths are difficult at best, impossible at worst. There is a huge borran earth high in the western Pennines and it is one of the worst places I have ever worked with a terrier. On two occasions I have had foxes to ground here and the terriers have worked them hard, but have been unable to get right up to their quarry. It is easy to tell when a terrier cannot reach a fox, due to a very tight tunnel, or a ledge that is just out of reach, for it will emerge after a time and look for a better way in. On both of these occasions the foxes would not bolt and that is not surprising. Such places are not easily dug and so Reynard will very often choose to remain below, especially if the terrier cannot quite get to it. It is such cunning tactics that make the hunting of foxes very difficult indeed, so control is not always an easy thing to carry out. Very often, the odds are stacked in favour of the fox.

When I began hunting an area, mainly of sheep farming, during the early nineties, it had not been hunted by hounds for some time and so quite a large population had developed and this was causing problems for both the shepherds and local wildlife. Lapwings, curlew, partridge, pheasant, put out by rough shooters, skylarks, snipe and woodcock; all numbers of these species had dropped dramatically and I was convinced it was due to the large population of foxes now inhabiting the area. So I began putting into operation a plan that would hopefully help with this situation. A couple of local farms had also lost large numbers of hens and things became more worrying when a pack of twelve foxes were seen hunting a narrow valley close to one of these farms.

I based my actions on hunting with hounds and decided to work coverts of bracken, gorse and heather, as well as reedbeds, or anywhere else a fox may use as sanctuary, employing the technique of dispersal that hunts use, which prevents foxes from living in packs. Along with this, I would work earths and dispatch those foxes that it was possible to do so. When I first began doing this, sometimes as many as six foxes were flushed by the terriers from just one small covert and they would be running all over the place. Before this, foxes were not using the earths at all, but once I started disturbing their daytime hideouts, they began going to ground and so I was able to account for quite a number of these by digging etc. And sometimes the terriers would manage to hold scent long enough to follow the fox to its chosen lair underground and then it would be accounted for. On occasion, they even caught foxes in covert.

After a few seasons of doing this, I soon began to notice a marked difference. Foxes were now never found in more than pairs, and even this was rare, for usually just the one would be found skulking in covert. Lamb losses were reduced and during one springtime there were none at all in this area, which was a massive improvement. Also, and best of all, numbers of ground-nesting birds have increased dramatically and partridge, curlew, lapwing, snipe and woodcock, as well as skylarks, are on the increase and are becoming far more common sights. Numbers are not as high as when I was a lad, but still there is a huge improvement and wildlife is much richer, due, I believe, to a fox control programme of reducing their numbers, but not of attempting to eliminate them. Foxes are wonderful creatures and I love to see them in our countryside, but not in such high numbers that it makes the health of another species suffer dramatically, as was happening in this area. The evidence all points to the fact that both farmers and local wildlife truly benefit when fox numbers are kept at a reasonably low level. If serious national surveys were carried out, that were truly unbiased and unprejudiced, then I am certain that those areas that are keepered, or where productive fox control is employed, would be found to be rich in wildlife, when compared to those places where foxes are allowed to thrive without check.

There is plenty of evidence that proves the need for controlling fox numbers and this chapter could go on and on with many examples, but one of the most compelling reasons for carrying out such control was highlighted dramatically during the most recent foot and mouth outbreak. Surveys were carried out and the findings were most interesting. Almost five thousand foxes were spared during that outbreak, which would normally have been culled otherwise. Almost five thousand calls were received during that time, from farmers who had lost livestock to foxes, sometimes in massive numbers. On average, the Welsh sheep farmers lost thirty lambs each during this outbreak and the cost, for each farmer, as one can imagine, ran into hundreds of pounds.

The same story could be told of many other areas such as the Lake District and the Scottish Borders. This survey was only carried out regarding hunts and gun packs, so the actual numbers were far higher when parts of the country that are not hunted are taken into consideration. In Wales alone, well over one hundred farms suffered severe lamb losses that far exceeded the norm, costing each farm at least an additional £500 in lost revenue. These figures speak for themselves. If the hunting and culling of foxes stopped abruptly and they became a protected species, which some lunatics would like to see happen, then the consequences for farmers would be disastrous. During this time, losses of chickens to foxes, as well as other livestock such as piglets and ducks, also increased dramatically up and down the country.

Anyone who has had any dealings with foxes will no doubt have a great respect for this wonderful creature. They are incredibly beautiful and the sight of a fox in full winter coat is a joy to behold. Fox watching is a great way of enjoying foxes in the privacy of their own little world and this is especially true when a breeding den is found and the rearing of the family is carefully studied. But still, as beautiful as they are and as enchanting as it is to watch them in their own environment, the truth of the matter is that the very

Paul Stead and Derek Webster with a fox dug using Gem. Derek's fox-catching lurcher was named Floss.

nature of foxes gives a compelling reason to control their numbers using methods that are as humane as possible. I for one, would quickly turn anti-hunting if the elimination of the fox was the goal aimed for, but this simply is not so. The reason for control is to maintain a healthy population, while at the same time providing a service to farmers, shepherds and gamekeepers, as well as protecting wildlife such as ground-nesting birds, which suffer greatly where large fox numbers are found. And, as if this wasn't enough, there is yet another good reason why fox control *must* be carried out.

Foxes suffer from diseases such as distemper and mange, both of which are spread by carriers and victims. Distemper is a terrible disease and a fox will suffer greatly until death at last relieves the torment. Mange, too, can be a killer. True, some foxes recover from mange, but only if they can find easy prey such as hens, or lambs, or, in the case of urban foxes, leftovers thrown on the floor, or hanging out of bins. A fox full of mange is in no state for catching its usual prey and so country foxes, which cannot scavenge in the same way as urban foxes can, will suffer far more and are more likely to die as a result of the illness. Many foxes die anyway after the badly scratched skin becomes infected and poisons the system, leading to organ failure, if starvation does not see them off first.

Whilst carrying out fox control, many sick foxes are found and killed each year by hounds, terriers and lurchers, and thus the suffering is ended very quickly. Also, when sick foxes are culled in this way, the opportunities for such diseases to spread are dramatically reduced and so a healthier population is maintained. The weak and the old are more likely to contract and spread disease, but, when hunted by hounds in particular, these will usually fall victim and thus the chances of diseases spreading, again, are dramatically reduced. When wolves prowled our countryside, one can be sure that those foxes that remained were the fittest of the bunch and the same can be said after a season of hunting with hounds. The weak, the old, the sick, all will have fallen victim to the pack and only the very fittest will then be left to breed. True, some of the older foxes will have survived by sheer cunning, but it is unlikely that such 'oldies' will survive the season to come. And the new crop of cubs will have the weak and sickly among them and these too, potential carriers of disease, will undoubtedly be sorted out when hunting resumes again at the back-end of summer. Or that is how things stood, until the ignorant and prejudiced stepped in and voted in favour of a law that makes things far worse, not better, for foxes in England, Wales and Scotland. If only folk would deal with their prejudice and blind sentiment and look at the facts that speak for themselves. Maybe then they will see how there is a real need to control fox numbers by using humane methods, including that of hounds, terriers and lurchers.

CHAPTER FOUR

TRADITIONAL METHODS: USING HOUNDS, TERRIERS AND LURCHERS

Hunting with Hounds

One of the main reasons for the use of hounds being the most selective and efficient way of controlling fox numbers, is because of their use when dealing with foxes which are killing lambs or poultry. Where losses occur, the farmer will notify the Huntsman of his local pack and then hounds will be taken to the fields where foxes are preying upon livestock and cast for the scent of the guilty party. Very often, that scent will be taken up and followed until the culprit is found and dealt with. This type of 'spring hunting' occurs up and down the country, but is used most effectively in mountainous areas such as Wales, the Lake District and Scotland. The fact that many of the Welsh packs are out seven days a week throughout much of the spring is an indication of how reliable they can be in tackling this problem, and of how much the farmers and shepherds rely on them.

This method of hunting, which operates in conjunction with hill farmers in the main, has always been popular in the Lake District and was practised long before John Peel made hunting in the fells much more popular, raising its profile to a sporting and social occasion, rather than just a means of controlling a pest. Indeed, John Peel himself, although having fixtures that ensured he covered a large area of country throughout the season, also employed this method and regularly answered the calls of farmers in his area who were experiencing losses of their livestock to marauding foxes. In those days foxes were few and far between, considered more as vermin than as a sporting beast, and thus harder to come across.

Maurice Bell and the Wensleydale Foxhounds in typical Dales hunting country. *(photo Robert Dent)*

And, because they were so few in number and were hunted relentlessly using all kinds of methods, it is possible that they were far more cunning too. Thus Peel had a job on his hands whenever he was called out to hunt down such foxes, but he had good working hounds that would stick to a line until doomsday if need be, and so he accounted for many in those days. Geese were popular around farmyards, for selling, feeding the family and producing goose grease that was once used for a variety of tasks around the farm, and so it is not surprising that many times Peel was called out to deal with a fox that had got in among the geese. More often than not, he returned with the culprit slung over his shoulder, which was then hung from a crook at a local inn, where celebrations usually continued until well into the early hours. Peel's ponies knew the country better than he himself and it was mostly thanks to them that he got home after one of his hunt celebrations. If it were not for these ponies, Peel may well have passed a frosty night under the stars, his beer-fumed breath billowing into the icy air, which no doubt would have ended in tragedy.

One of the most exciting of these kind of hunts, a 'lambing call', as they are known in the fells, occurred when Jim Dalton was Huntsman of the Blencathra Foxhounds. A farmer in the Keswick area had been losing lambs and Dalton was quickly informed. During the previous afternoon, he gathered a few couple of hounds, a brace or two of coupled terriers, and set off over the fells and arrived at the farm in plenty of time to feed and bed-down his pack and the brave, hardy terriers too. Nowadays, it is much easier with transport being available to get hounds about country quickly, but back then it was all done on foot and so Dalton would need to travel to the place where losses occurred the day before and stay there for the night, enjoying the hospitality of the farmers in his area. The farmers highly respected the Huntsman and his Whipper-in and loved to have them stay over for the night, enjoying a great social occasion as well as a means of protecting their flocks. This would undoubtedly relieve the isolation of many of these farms that were far from any village or town.

Dalton was up early, well before dawn, on that spring morning all those years ago, and got his pack ready. As soon as dawn began to relieve the pitch-blackness, hounds were loosed from their kennel and taken around the pastures full of lambs. A drag was taken up and hounds were soon away to nearby Walla Crag. There are some huge crags in this area and plenty of coverts lie below them, so it wasn't long before they had their fox afoot. The music of the pack grew louder and echoed among the vast rising crags, ringing throughout the woods as they pursued their quarry, sticking to the line of their foe as it led them along the steep wooded hillsides that are incredibly difficult to negotiate. Hounds went away along Barrowside and on through Ashness Gill. This area is one of the most photographed of all the beauty spots in the Lakes and the views from here are terrific. However, with hounds hot on the trail, Dalton had little time for admiring views!

Hounds began to struggle now as the fox led them out onto open fell and he easily put a lot of ground 'twixt himself and the oncoming pack. Close to Watendlath, where the famed Blencathra Huntsman, Johnny Richardson, was born and raised, the fox lay down deep inside a plantation, in the hopes that he had foiled the hunt. The thieving fox, however, soon discovered how persistent a pack of hounds can be, as they entered the plantation, eagerly searching for the quarry they knew to be hiding somewhere here-abouts. With the pressure now well and truly on, Reynard at last broke cover and began climbing out onto the higher fells, firstly taking hounds over High Seat at almost two thousand feet, and then away across the wild, wide-open fell to Armboth, the view of Thirlmere Lake now before them.

He now crossed to Armboth fell and then headed for Raven Crag, crossing the rough screes above Thirlmere and managing, once again, to gain quite a bit of ground on the pack. Fell hounds are experts at covering rough ground such as a scree-covered fell-side, but they cannot match a fox over such hard country. Foxes fairly fly across even the roughest of ground and crossing scree and borrans, or climbing crags, is a tactic regularly employed in the fells, which often succeeds, in the end, in throwing off the pack. Reynard now remained in country at the head of Thirlmere and eluded capture as he went through rock, scree, crag and woodland, yet still they came, working out his line and baying amongst the fells as they continued on, working hard and being encouraged by the Huntsman and followers. The pack had hunted this thieving fox in the past and he often got to Worm Crag and lost hounds amongst the vast outcrops of rock and deep heather, but hounds were now gaining fast as Reynard passed over Smeathwaite in the direction of the crags, forcing him to turn down Williams Ghyll instead.

He crossed Naddle Valley and climbed out onto Causeway Pike, again crossing some of the roughest country to be found in the fells, huge crags with scree scattered all across the incredibly steep and dangerous fellsides, as well as wooded areas where the fox was well hidden from view. This is some of the most picturesque of all the Lake District scenery and the views here are terrific. I have hunted this very same area with the Blencathra Foxhounds and have been stunned at the country they hunt, which is dramatic, awesome and incredibly beautiful. However, this hunt was hotting up very much indeed and both fox and hounds had put in a lot of hard work and a lot of ground had been covered, so followers were intent on keeping with hounds. The cry of hounds rose now, and the pace quickened as they closed the gap, despite the best efforts and cunning of this game fox. Dropping down over the other side, the fox now took hounds into Great Wood, almost where the hunt had begun, and then headed out onto open fell again, crossing the mosses and going out across Bleaberry fell, hoping to make for the crags where he was intent on hiding from hounds, but they pressed him so hard that he was forced to turn and make for The Benn instead. Here he went to ground in a huge borran earth that was difficult to work.

Jim Dalton was not only a great houndsman, but he was also one of the greatest of all the terrier breeders the Lakes has ever produced, creating his own strain of terrier that was unbeatable at work. They were also typey and won well at shows, but it was working qualities that made them famous. Especially were they excellent finders and stayers, for the Blencathra country contains massive borrans and only the best terriers can work such places successfully. Dalton's proved to be of the very best and regularly worked such vast, impossible earths. True, Dalton smartened up his rough and ready strain of fell terrier by using Fox terrier blood which was readily available at The Carlisle and District Otterhounds kennels; terriers descended from those of John Russell, the hunting parson himself, but still, they were far from 'show' terriers. Two of these terriers, Pincher and Banter, were now entered into this borran, which hounds were marking keenly when Dalton arrived with his coupled earth dogs. Although these terriers could do the job alone, if need be, it was necessary to enter two at a time, simply because of the size of this borran. A fox can easily dodge a lone terrier in such a vast place, but not so a brace of determined workers.

Pincher and Banter searched every nook and cranny they came across, testing the air around that borran, and eventually found their foe as it hid among the huge boulders of immovable rock, hundreds of tons in weight. This brace of terriers, as was the case with most of Dalton's earth dogs, were fox killers and so, finding things a little too heated below ground, Reynard eventually bolted and fled from the noisy, belligerent pair. He now climbed out to the top of The Benn and the lead hounds, Comely, Stormer and Charmer, weren't far behind. He was being hard pressed once more and both fox and hounds were tiring after such a long and hard hunt. The fox now descended the fell and crossed Naddle Bottoms and headed out onto High Rigg above St John's in the Vale, where, at last, hounds caught up with him and ended his

Hounds heading for the fells.

crimes forever. It had been a long, hard hunt, but one that had demonstrated the value of a pack of hounds to a farming community. A fell fox had been worrying lambs, a fox that had committed such crimes in the past and one that had been hunted unsuccessfully before this time, but now those crimes had brought justice at last.

Hunting with hounds in places such as the English Lake District is, out of necessity, carried out on foot. The hounds used in such mountainous districts tend to be lighter boned than those used for work in the shires and they also need to show more intelligence, being self-reliant, for very often the Huntsman can do nothing to help should a check occur. A check happens when scent is lost and the mounted Huntsman will usually 'lift' hounds' noses and move them on to where he thinks his fox has gone, picking up the scent again and resuming the hunt. In the fells, the Huntsman may still be in the valley that hounds left behind quite some time ago, so they must then put *themselves* right. One of the most impressive sights to see when hunting with a foot pack, is that of hounds working a crag. Reynard will very often climb a crag expertly, leaving hounds at the foot of the rocks and making for ground that is impossible for the pack to negotiate, thus he cannot be followed. Sometimes Reynard will lie on a narrow ledge and refuse to budge, and thus save his brush for that day, or he will climb out at the top and carry on his travels across the fells. It is then that one can witness the intelligence of a pack of fell hounds.

In most cases, the pack will split and a few couple will go to the left, a few to the right, and they will then climb up each side of the crag and meet at the top, very often where the fox has left the crag for open fell. Exactly how hounds have come to know how to do this is difficult to explain, but I would say that, during those early days of fell hunting hundreds of years ago, the Huntsmen and Whips would each take a few hounds up the sides of these crags where hounds had been unable to follow and then a line would have been struck at the top of the crag. Hounds catch on very quickly and so the more experienced would then teach the young entry how to sort out the scent of a 'cragged' fox, passing this down from generation to generation until the present day. Once learnt, the Huntsman and his Whip would have no need to interfere whenever a fox took to the crags. Of course, not all foxes leave a crag at the top. Some will find a ledge and stay put. In this situation a hound will sometimes climb out to its fox, or, indeed, a terrier, though some will come to grief while attempting to reach their quarry, falling from the crag onto the rocks far below. If a Huntsman is up with his pack when a fox 'binks' on a crag, especially if it is a notoriously dangerous place such as the Honister Crag which has claimed the lives of many hounds, then he will call hounds off and draw for another, not wishing to risk the lives of his gallant pack.

Hunting with hounds in the fells is far more difficult than in the shires and foxes are far harder to catch, due to the hostile nature of the terrain, as well as the agility, stamina and cunning of hill foxes. Foxes are far more suited to such landscapes, than either hounds or terriers, and so man has produced working terriers and hounds that are the best it is possible to produce. The lighter-boned fell hound and the game Fell, or Lakeland, terrier, are well adapted to working this incredibly difficult region, but still, the odds are stacked in Reynard's favour. The same can be said of foot packs in

Scotland, Wales and Ireland, which hunt mountainous districts in the main.

I was out one day with a small team of hounds and we were hunting across a bleak, rock-strewn fellside where deep heather made the going difficult, to say the least. Hounds cast around all over the place and hunted a cold drag or two, but otherwise there was little about, the old scents soon fading until they were lost forever. It was late November and the autumn winds held the icy tinge of the coming winter and so hunting at a thousand feet and more, was really quite cold, as you can imagine. The pack drew over rock and scree and heather which still held the dead flowers of late summer that had once bloomed brilliant purple, now looking morose in that awful dull-brown colouring, the withered blooms falling to the ground as the pack brushed through the dense cover. They then worked below a crag and eventually headed for the cold rocks above, which jutted out close to the top of the fell. Hounds tested every entrance and at last began marking eagerly. There were plenty of rabbit droppings all over the place and so we hoped they hadn't gone wrong.

Fell was entered into this rock earth and it wasn't long before he found his quarry and began immediately working it hard. This earth is a difficult spot and quite impossible to dig, so, as you can imagine, that fox was not keen on the idea of vacating the premises. In fact, it was determined to stay put and so Fell had a job on his hands to shift it. However, he is a determined worker and leaves no space 'twixt himself and his quarry, working close and hard and unrelenting, and so, in the end, after about twenty minutes of baying at, and tackling, his quarry, the fox finally decided to make for open ground and Fell succeeded in evicting the tenant from this fortress earth. A big dog fox, unmistakable with its size and broad head, shot out of a gap in the rocks at speed, only a few feet from where I stood, and immediately made for the roughest ground possible. The rock and scree below the crags was the place it now sped across, hardly hindered by the rough terrain, with hounds in pursuit. However, the ground here is incredibly difficult and it took the pack far longer to cross it as they first hunted by sight, and then, as the fox dropped off the rocks and into the dense ling, disappearing from view, by scent.

Although we followed as best we could across that rough terrain,

I kept one eye on that fox as it sped across rough scrub-pastures on the top of a hill and then dropped down into a valley, now completely out of sight. Hounds took up the line expertly and scent proved quite good as they followed it through the heather, out onto a dirt track that winds its way into the fells, and then onto the reed-covered pastures on top of a lower hill. They screamed and bayed with excitement as they disappeared over the crest of the hill and began dropping down into the valley which was wooded and well covered with the russet-bracken beds growing all over the place, alongside thick gorse and bramble bushes. We made it to the top of the hill and watched from here as the few hounds hunted their quarry down into the valley bottom and began ascending the hill on the other side, slowly, slowly, following the line, which wasn't quite as keen as it had been. It had been very wet of late and so scent, on the waterlogged ground, failed to lie well. But still, the determined hounds pressed onwards and kept with the scent all the way into the next valley where, a little later, scent was at last lost for good. It had been an exciting hunt and Fell had 'bossed' his quarry in fine

Hounds drawing for their quarry.

style, eventually 'persuading' it to shift from its sanctuary. Hounds had hunted well, despite the difficult landscape and weather conditions. It had been a hunt that well demonstrates the advantage foxes have in fell country. Not that they are a pushover in the shires, far from it in fact.

Mounted hunting is not an easy way of controlling fox numbers, but still it is very effective in accounting for the weak, the sick and the old, in any hunt country. If surveys were carried out, analysing areas that are hunted and comparing them with those that are not, then I am certain that the results would show that the healthiest foxes were those living in country that is hunted over. True, hunting with hounds, whether it be in the shires, or up in the fells, does not account for large numbers of foxes in any given season, but that does not mean that such methods are not effective. Shooting accounts for far more and a gun pack will account for as many as three hundred foxes during an average season, over three times the amount accounted for by a pack of hounds hunted in the more traditional way, but shooting is indiscriminate and the healthy and strong will die alongside the weak, sick and the old. If hounds enter a covert and there is a sick beast in that covert, very often that will be the one accounted for, usually 'chopped' very quickly, with the pack then going on to hunt and *maybe* kill a healthier specimen. When hounds flush foxes from a covert, very often all will be shot. So hunting with hounds is selective and helps maintain a strong, healthy population. If, in the spring, lambs are killed, then those hounds can be brought in to deal with the guilty party, rather than indiscriminately killing several foxes and possibly failing to catch up with the actual culprit, which can occur when using the gun, or other methods. So in this type of situation it can be said that hunting with hounds is *the* most efficient way of keeping fox numbers at reasonable levels, which benefits both farm livestock and wildlife in general.

In fact, hunting with hounds provides much more than a service to farmers who have livestock to protect; it is also an important way in which much of our countryside, along with its invaluable habitats for wildlife, is protected. For instance, hunts plant coverts ranging from large tracts of woodland, to areas full of gorse, or bramble bushes. These areas are then managed in order to provide habitat for foxes that is at its best and this, in turn, will then benefit many other species of insects, birds and mammals. Hedges are laid, woodland coppiced, and areas left to the wild, where large tracts of wildflowers thrive during the spring, summer and autumn months. Many of the coverts are important sights for bluebells, harebells and other wild blooms that must be protected if we are not to lose them from our precious countryside.

The booklet, *Hunting – The Facts*, published by the organisation now known as The Countryside Alliance is a very interesting publication that presents the facts in a simple and honest way and it has much to say on conservation matters that are promoted by hunting. It tells us that in the country of the Warwickshire Hunt, at the time of publication, fifty-five woodlands had been planted specifically for foxes to use and that just seven of these together will cover hundreds of acres. It has this to say in the conclusion of the section on conservation; 'The hunt plays a large part in keeping local bridleways open, maintaining hedges and fences, and clearing and managing woodland. The hunt also encourages traditional laying of hedges and management of coverts, making an attractive habitat for wildlife of all kinds.' Those who oppose hunting and wish to see it disappear forever from our countryside, cannot see the wood for the trees, so to speak.

To hunt foxes using hounds means to preserve foxes and their habitat, which then benefits other species greatly. And, because fox numbers are kept to reasonable levels in any hunt country, other wildlife species can thrive as there are not large numbers of foxes preying on them. Removing the hunting of foxes with hounds is a sure way to see harm come to our countryside in many different ways, through neglect of wooded areas and other coverts, as well as the potential to see fox numbers either decline dramatically due to less selective methods of control, as was the case in earlier centuries, or the massive increase of fox numbers that will see the animals packing and becoming even more of a nuisance to farmers, especially in this day and age of free-range farming, when piglets and chickens in particular are already preyed upon on a regular basis.

Of course, if hounds are hunted just for 'sport', in order to give the field a day out riding, then this, apart from the benefits of conservation, is of little use to anyone. A pack of hounds in any hunt country should provide an effective pest control service to farmers, whichever country they hunt, whether it be Ireland, America, France, Australia, or any other country where this form of hunting is carried out. Any pack that does not take pest control seriously is in grave danger of providing anti-hunt organisations with ammunition that can be effectively used against them. And we know of the outcome in the British Isles. The image of 'sport' and the lack of will to control fox numbers effectively by some hunts, however few they may have been, added fuel to the fire in the campaign against hunting and no doubt played some part in getting it banned. Hunts in other countries should learn from this, making certain that they can be called upon at any time in order to deal with a fox that is killing livestock. The conservation of hunt countries and the associated benefits to wildlife should be publicly promoted and the emphasis placed on pest control and not 'sport'. Hunting, in whatever country it takes place, must move with the times and completely change its image, if it is to survive the plague of 'political correctness'. In view of what has happened in the British Isles, it may be shrewd of the hunting world to sit up and take note and take steps now to completely change the image of hunting. It is no good hanging onto tradition, if that tradition brings fierce opposition that can do away with such activities. Steps taken now, in order to preserve hunting with hounds, would be steps well taken, no matter how much of 'the tradition' has to be done away with in order for that preservation to be accomplished.

For instance, the Huntsman and Whip must be seen as separate from the field in general. The public perception is of two men in scarlet jackets being there to provide as long a hunt as possible for the riders following. The public should be educated to understand that the Huntsman and Whipper-in are there first and foremost to provide a service to the local farming community, keeping the fox population down to a reasonable level, in order that livestock and wildlife can thrive. The followers are there to observe serious pest control being carried out, while at the same time enjoying a spectacular ride across beautiful countryside. Remember, the perception of hunting being a 'sport' is what has turned so many against it and every effort should be made to move away from this image.

Foxhunting was undoubtedly carried out in Roman times, and

The Holcombe hounds heading for the first draw.

probably earlier, but it was the English who made it popular and developed it into what has become an art form, particularly from the early eighteenth century onwards. Tastes, of course, have changed since that time and the trend moved away from slow hounds that would work out a cold drag for hours, before actually finding a fox, as is the way of fell packs, especially during Peel's day, to fast-paced hounds that can lead the mounted field across large tracts of countryside in quick bursts of speed. This faster hunting, however, has its drawbacks. For one thing, the mounted field miss a lot of fine hound work as they work out a line meticulously. Maurice Bell's Wensleydale Foxhounds are noted for their ability to work out a cold drag, more or less unaided, Maurice having built up an independent pack, and one can see some wonderful work whilst out with such hounds. But fast-paced hunting leaves the mounted field, for the most part, far behind and the fast-disappearing pack is usually the impression left on the field.

During the seventeenth century, foxhunting, or the foxhunting tradition, left English shores and in 1650 Robert Brooke arrived in Maryland, America, with his family and his hounds. Other settlers also took hounds with them to this newly discovered country and hunts were set up in different regions, growing in popularity and spreading through the eighteenth century until it was well established, particularly in Maryland and Virginia. I suspect, however, that a variety of quarry was hunted during those early times and not just foxes, including coyotes, bobcats, wild pigs and no doubt other beasts such as American badgers and racoons. Do not forget, many of the early packs in England hunted a variety of quarry and hares, badgers, stoats and polecats were hunted alongside the more fashionable fox.

Foxhunting, or the foxhunting tradition, has spread throughout many American states and has also reached Canada. Foxhunting with hounds also takes place in France, though many of these are foot packs and they will hunt rabbits and hares, even deer, as eagerly as they will hunt the fox. Italy has a growing tradition of hunting with hounds and packs have also been formed and are being hunted in South Africa. They are growing in popularity for sure, but no doubt the anti-brigade will also grow in these countries, and I say take a lesson from English, Scottish and Welsh foxhunting. Do not make the mistake of thinking that it can never be banned in your country. Take action now to improve public image in order to combat that opposition, before it is too late. In my opinion, if getting rid of the scarlet jacket would make hunting with hounds more acceptable, then get rid. Some other bright colour will do the job just as effectively and I would rather wear lime-green, than scarlet, if I thought that would bring less opposition.

Using terriers

Hunting with hounds is incredibly exciting and hunting the fox in particular is very challenging indeed, but for that hunting to be both an exciting day out in the countryside, and an effective means of controlling a predator that can cause very much damage when in among livestock, or wildlife such as ground-nesting birds, terriers are necessary to any pack, for effective control would not be possible without them. And it was the earth-stopper, as well as

Terriers are essential for bolting foxes from impenetrable rockpiles such as this one in the Yorkshire Dales.

the hunt terrierman, who prized them most. In more recent years the earth-stopper and terrierman are one and the same person, but in days gone by they were very often two separate people enjoying two separate roles at the hunt. Earth-stoppers of old were local countrymen who lived an almost nomadic life, wandering about the countryside during the hours of darkness, and in all weathers, and blocking up earths within a few miles radius of where the meet would take place on the following morning. These countrymen would have known every earth and badger sett in the area and all would have been blocked before daylight set in. The earth-stopper would also have been consulted by the Huntsman *before* hunting actually began, and often while it was taking place, enquiring if any foxes had been seen entering any of the local coverts. Information gleaned from these men, who had a vast knowledge of wildlife in general, and of every aspect of the hunt country, was invaluable information which would help the Huntsman quickly locate a fox, which became the fashion after the 'working out a cold drag' days were over. In fact, many Huntsmen built fine reputations on the information they got from earth-stoppers, information that would help quickly locate foxes, which was essential in some hunt countries, if the Master and field were to be kept happy.

The earth-stopper would wander about the countryside throughout the night, either on foot, or, more likely, on a pony, with a brace or two of terriers taken along in order to ensure that any earths blocked were not occupied. During the hours of darkness it is unlikely that earths would have any occupants, but that is not always the case. Sometimes a fox will take its kill below ground during the night and eat it there, so it is reasonable to assume that those terriers would be used, even at night, in order to evict any foxes found at home. And then, by the light of an oil lantern, the earth would be blocked and some potent mixture poured around the entrance in order to prevent the fox, or badger, from digging back in. Urinating on the blockage would produce the same result, but producing enough with which to spray every earth and badger sett within the hunt country would be an absolute impossibility, unless, of course, one took a coach-load of drunks along who had enjoyed a day at the races on an organised pub outing! Many hunts had such earth-stoppers available and in earlier times, when much of our land belonged to the gentry and all country estates had gamekeepers, any keepered land to be hunted over would be 'stopped' by the keepers themselves, who, of course, would know of every fox earth and badger sett on their beat.

The terriers belonging to these earth-stoppers would of necessity be game, but they would need much sense and must never attack a fox, just stand off and bay, evicting the quarry in order that the earth could be blocked in preparation of a day's hunting to come. The last thing an earth-stopper would want is a hard terrier that would attack its foe and either kill it below, or drive it out of the earth inflicted with injuries. That fox, if found by hounds, would probably not last for very long and so a long hunt would not ensue. If a fox would not bolt, then the earth-stopper would be required to dig it out and send it on its way, thus his terriers would need to be 'stayers', that is, they must not leave their fox, but stay with it until dug out by their master. These terriers belonging to both earth-stoppers and terriermen were incredibly game little dogs that would be superb finders, marking earths as occupied, or otherwise, by simply testing scent at the entrance. They would then need to find the quarry and work it hard, but without actually attacking their foe, simply barking, nipping and teasing until Reynard fled the scene. If the fox refused to bolt, then they would need to hold the fox in the same place until the master dug them out and let the fox go. And all of this during the hours of darkness. Or is that really the case?

Well, in some instances, yes. Wentworth, of Castle Howard near York, was one of those old earth-stoppers who did much of his work under cover of darkness, roaming the countryside on his pony and blocking the earths that were marked as occupied, or otherwise, by a brace of terriers he always had with him. And then, after hunting had finished, he would go around unblocking the earths

Terriers are the only effective way of bolting foxes from earths.

during the night following the hunt. But not all carried out their work in this manner, for some would earth-stop during the afternoon prior to the next morning's hunting. This was true in former times, but more so in recent decades when this form of earth-stopping became more popular. I know an old Huntsman who was once the Whipper-in to a pack of hounds which hunt close to the foot of the Highlands in Scotland, and have enjoyed many interesting conversations with him, especially of his days spent earth-stopping for the hunt.

This was always carried out during the afternoon of the day before hunting was to take place and he said that the terriers employed at that hunt, the Fife Foxhounds, were incredibly game. They bolted many, many foxes during those afternoon forays, but on numerous occasions the fox would not bolt and had to be dug out and forcibly evicted. And thus, before any actual hunting took place, those terriers had already put in a lot of graft, yet they were still incredibly keen to go if they were needed during the following day's hunting (foxes are unpredictable and sometimes take hounds great distances, well away from the area that had been 'stopped', and so terriers would still be required in such cases). Sometimes though, badgers were found skulking in a fox earth and on several occasions an afternoon's earth-stopping turned into a hard day's badger digging (digging badgers was legal in those days), for, as the Huntsman said, there was no other way of retrieving the terriers. They came to no harm, for they would stand off and bay, cleverly teasing their quarry and holding it until dug out, but they would not come off their foe, no matter how much their master called them. And so, in the end, there was no other option but to dig. These terriers were white bodied and they may well have been descended, in part, from the terriers of John Russell himself, for his Fox terriers certainly worked with the Fife Foxhounds during the nineteenth century and would undoubtedly have had some influence on local terrier strains, for they were amongst the very gamest workers of the time. Whatever their breeding, they were certainly game stock that could find, bolt their quarry, or stay until dug out if necessary. In more recent decades I would say that the vast majority of earth-stopping has been carried out during daylight hours, rather than during the night, which was certainly the fashion of earlier times, particularly during the eighteenth and nineteenth centuries. And, in more recent times, the terrierman has fulfilled both roles, as earth-stopper and hunt terrierman, rather than there being two separate men employed by the hunt, as was usually the case in bygone times. But still, I cannot help wondering just how necessary earth-stopping really is, especially after my forays with several of the fell packs.

Earth-stopping is certainly necessary regarding badger setts, for foxes will use these as a means of escape when hard-pressed by hounds. So there is certainly no question of the necessity of this practice in certain areas, but when it comes to the hunting of foxes, many will remain above ground and long hunts result, despite the fact that the quarry can get into an earth at any time it chooses. This is true when a fox runs some distance and is soon out of the country that has been 'stopped', but it is also true in hilly and mountainous districts where earth-stopping is an impossibility, due to the nature of the terrain and large rock earths that simply cannot be blocked. This is especially so in places such as North Yorkshire and the Lake District. Foxes can cover such vast areas in these places that earth-stopping becomes a complete waste of time anyway. And attempting to block borrans would end in frustration and failure. Despite this, many game foxes are found and hunted and these show little, if any, inclination to go to ground. Of course, at other times they do disappear below and that is why terriers have played such an important part in hunting on the fells, indeed, hunting without them would be a complete waste of time. Hunting foxes in these mountainous areas is incredibly sporting and far more exciting than hunting with a shire pack, yet no earth-stopping is practised, which raises the question as to exactly how necessary it really is, except, as already stated, in the case of badger setts where terriers cannot be entered, or it is unwise to do so, due to the size and depth of such places.

Packs that carry out serious fox control, rather than being concerned with a 'sporting' day out and attempting to keep a fox above ground just so that it can be hunted for as long as possible, may not concern themselves with earth-stopping, for there are terriermen who can deal with any foxes that will not bolt from any earths they enter. If the landowner, or local farmers, want the fox to be despatched, then it should be dug out and shot. Where earth-stopping is not practised there will always be found game foxes that will not rush to the first earth they come across and shoot below ground. Some foxes in the fells will remain above ground and sometimes provide a hunt that will last for much of the day, even into the darkness of the evening, despite the fact that there are a hundred and one places into which it could creep for sanctuary.

Earth-stopping has been one of the practices that has fuelled the growing opposition to hunting, as many folk cannot accept that keeping a fox above ground in order that a long hunt can be enjoyed is really about pest control. And one can understand this viewpoint. Fox control will be more effective when a fox does go to ground, for then it can be dug out using terriers and then shot. So to argue that earth-stopping aids pest control is a very weak argument indeed. The hunting ban in England and Wales has now made such a practice illegal (stopping badger setts), and unnecessary. Fox hunts in other countries may wish to learn from this. Take Ireland as an example. Opposition to hunting is growing on the Emerald Isle and its very existence may be in real danger in just a few years time (unless the ban in England and Wales is overturned in the courts, which would mean that hunting will no longer be a political issue) and so taking steps now to break down that opposition may well be necessary. One way in which fox control, rather than 'sport', can be emphasised is to do away with earth-stopping, except with regard to badger setts in the area, and allow terriermen to deal with those foxes that do go to ground, especially if livestock has been preyed upon in that district. If steps such as this were taken, then I am sure that most reasonable folk, if they thought that hunts were taking predator control more seriously, rather than concentrating on a 'sporting' day out, would not oppose hunting with hounds.

I have had many discussions with people from wide-ranging backgrounds and all share one thing in common – they cannot accept that it is right to hunt a fox for miles in order that the mounted field can enjoy a day out riding to hounds. Earth-stopping has only added to this image of cruelty and torture and this has undoubtedly contributed to the success of getting hunting with hounds banned in England and Wales. If earth-stopping was no longer practised in those countries where hunting with hounds remains legal, then I am sure that some of the prejudice would be broken down and eliminated. Hunting with hounds needs to be

A fox dug in Derbyshire during the 1970s.

looked at closely and any methods that are questionable must be done away with, if hunting with hounds is to have any future at all, for one thing is certain – opposition will continue to grow and a ban *will* be sought in every country where this form of hunting takes place. For instance, in Australia, the fox, introduced by foxhunters in the first place, has become a real menace and many species of small rodent are now on the verge of extinction due to Reynard's predations. Hunts are seen as the heroes in this case, for they are hunting the beast that has been demonised 'down under'. But if hunts in this country then practised earth-stopping in order that the fox could be kept above ground and thus providing the field with a long, hard run, or a fox that went to ground was left for another day, without any attempt to account for it, then ammunition would be dealt out to the opposers of hunting and it wouldn't take long to convince the public and the politicians that hunting with hounds was actually preserving foxes, rather than reducing their numbers. So foxhunters in Australia, or any other country for that matter, must be serious about providing a fox control service that is both readily available and truly efficient. Reasonable people will accept that the hunting of foxes is necessary in order to control their numbers, I have found, but they cannot come to terms with the idea of hunting just for the sake of sport; an image all foxhunters must distance themselves from if this form of control is to survive.

I firmly believe that fox control would increase in efficiency when earth-stopping is not practised and I also believe that this would in no way affect the quality of the hunting. True, some foxes will not run far, but there will always be a good number that will remain above ground and give hounds a terrific run. This is true in the fells and so will hold good throughout any hunt country where foxhunting in the traditional way is still practised. One of the most exciting of hunts took place around Skiddaw during Jim Dalton's incredibly successful reign and, although the fells are full of rock-piles and crag earths, no terriers were needed on this occasion, despite five foxes being taken from those frozen, misty slopes.

Dalton took his pack onto Orthwaite Fell on that freezing February morning and a line was soon struck, the music of the pack rapidly swelling in volume as they unkennelled their quarry out on the wild, windswept slopes of the Cockup fells. This is not particularly high country, when compared with other Lake District fells, but still, this is truly wild country and a spectacular place to see hounds hunting their fox. The pack had hunted the drag well and they now pressed their fox hard as they pursued it, sometimes by sight, but, more often than not, by scent, out onto the higher Burn Tod, now forcing it to swing right, over White House and onto Dash, where the fox was caught by the fast-paced pack. It had not been a particularly long hunt, but still it had been incredibly exciting as hounds pursued their quarry across the rough, bleak fells that were covered in frost and traces of snow.

Hunting had begun on the Uldale fells, but Dalton now headed towards the Skiddaw range, which holds some of the bleakest and wildest country imaginable. Hounds cast around Dead Crags at the back of Skiddaw Forest and a second fox was soon afoot, making straightaway for Skiddaw Heights, where he lingered, possibly hoping to get to ground in a big rough spot, but hounds pressured

A terrier emerging from an earth.

him and he was forced on through Gibraltar and out onto the tops where the icy wind made the going difficult to say the least. Nevertheless, now covering the bleak tops where the grouse feed on the young heather shoots in the spring and summer months, hounds pressed on and soon caught up with their quarry, killing it behind Skiddaw House.

Heading back over the tops, Dalton now drew around the crags on Lonscale Fell and a third fox was quickly roused from its cold sleeping place. It took hounds across Skiddaw Breast and down Sawmill Ghyll and onto Mirehouse where fox number three died. It had been a fast hunt and hounds had left most of the followers behind, who were still high on the fell tops above. It was just as hounds caught up with their third fox that the weather really turned nasty. A gale had got up and now snow began to fall, which meant, of course, blizzard conditions that forced the hunters down from the higher slopes. Three foxes had been accounted for already and one would imagine that it would be time to head off to a nearby public house for celebrations and a bit of warmth and comfort, but these fell huntsmen are made of stern stuff and Dalton carried on regardless, now drawing the lower slopes around Skiddaw, the mountain that featured regularly in the hunts of John Peel.

Whilst drawing on the slopes just above Bassenthwaite, hounds put two foxes up and the pack now split. The fourth fox took them a merry dance all over the lower slopes of Skiddaw and was eventually caught, after about an hour or so, close to Applethwaite. This fourth fox was known to the hunters and had been hunted quite a few times before, always getting away around the Applethwaite area, but this time his luck had run out and he perished on that freezing, snow-covered morning. The music of the pack had rung around those hills and valleys for most of the day and it continued now, as fox number five was hunted by the other half of the pack. This fox climbed out onto Bassenthwaite Common and it was thought he was heading out onto the bleak, frozen fell tops where he would likely secure his brush in such awful conditions, but, again, hounds pressed him hard and turned him down Barkbethdale, chasing him into the village below, the fox taking shelter in the school yard where the children were out at play. Romer found his quarry and pulled it out, killing it quickly.

The followers that day were few in number and hounds must work independently when out on those exposed fells with virtually nobody to help when they get into trouble. The conditions were incredibly difficult and there were a hundred and more places where any of those foxes could have got to ground, yet exciting hunts resulted and all five foxes were taken that day. And this is not an isolated event in the fells. Tommy Graves, a keen lifelong follower of the Coniston Foxhounds, once told me of a hunt on Loughrigg Fell, which overlooks Ambleside, when, again, five foxes were taken in just one day's hunting.

Foxes seem to know when scenting conditions are bad, almost teasing the pack as they struggle to follow its line, yet fleeing rapidly when conditions are good. The same is true in certain hunted areas. A fox seems to know when a pack is having great difficulties and they are thus reluctant to head out into open country. This is especially true of wooded areas and forestry in particular. Hounds can be literally given the run around all day in such places and I have been out with hounds and seen them having to be called out of a wood, or forest, simply because they could not get their quarry out into more accessible areas where the hunt could have been more even. I was out with the Lunesdale

Locators are essential when digging to terriers.

Foxhounds when they were hunting wooded areas not far from Milnthorpe and actually catching those foxes was incredibly difficult, even nigh on impossible. These woods are well foxed and severe problems ensue when these places are used by shooting syndicates for the rearing of pheasant.

Foxes thrive in such areas simply because of the large pheasant population that provides plenty of food for them, especially when it comes to rearing cubs throughout the spring and summer months. And so a control policy is essential if losses are to be kept minimal. Once the shooting is over, hounds are allowed into these areas and they usually find very quickly. Sometimes several foxes are found and the pack can split into two or three different factions and keeping up with any one of them can be extremely difficult, when their music is echoing through the trees from all different directions. This is what happened on this particular day. Two or three foxes were flushed and the pack split, with their music coming from all over the place. We followed as best we could, up onto the higher ground, climbing the Fairy Steps, a natural rock formation, out onto the rocky plateau above and catching glimpses now and then of a few hounds as they pursued their quarry round and round the dense coverts, with literally hundreds of pheasants all over the area. At one spot, I loosed Mist and Fell from the leash, leaving them coupled while I ate a bit of breakfast, but a few minutes later a fox came running through the wood and the terriers were after it instantly, deafening out my cries to return until they had lost the scent somewhere in the distance. Just a couple of hounds were hunting this fox, so how many were actually afoot I do not know.

Eventually, after quite a lot of work from the Huntsman, most of the pack were gathered as one body onto just the one fox and now they were able to put the pressure on. The fox, by the afternoon, finally broke cover and headed across the rich green pastures where it went to ground in a small patch of woodland in the lower valley. A hunt terrier was put in and baying was soon heard, with the fox finally bolting and heading over the hill and into another earth, which proved to be an impossible place and so, in the end, that fox was given best. So, in some places, even with terriers at their disposal, hunting with a pack of hounds is not always effectual.

I believe that hunting with hounds is *the* most efficient way of controlling foxes in that it is usually the weak, the sick and the old that perish, and because, when lambs or other forms of farm live- stock are being taken, the guilty party can be dealt with by hounds taking up the scent and following it until that fox is accounted for. Also, dispersal occurs when coverts are disturbed and this prevents 'packing'. But there are also certain situations in which hunting with hounds, as we have seen, is not effective at all, such as in large, dense woodland and forestry. Also, with increasingly busy roads and building programmes encroaching more and more into our uniquely beautiful countryside, this form of fox control is im- possible to implement, hence there is a need for other methods too. Those in the hunting fraternity who think that foxes should be preserved for the sole purpose of being hunted by hounds are simply living in the past. Our modern landscape makes other forms of control absolutely essential and these can be far more effective when it comes to the numbers game, but it has to be said that all other methods are far less selective than the hunting of foxes with hounds. Digging with terriers, fast running lurchers and the deadly gun, will take healthy foxes just as easily as they will take sick, old, or weak ones, while the majority of healthy foxes will escape hounds, if they remain above ground, or get into an impossible earth that cannot be worked using the terriers.

Terriers play an important part in hunting with hounds, as we have seen, but they are also useful for hunting those areas where it is impossible to take hounds. For instance, a few years ago a farmer close to the M6 motorway was losing quite a number of lambs to a fox that was preying upon them. Because of the close proximity of the M6, this country was out of bounds to the local hunt and so the terrier and lurcher lads were called in. They dug, bolted and caught quite a number of foxes in that area and eventually caught up with the culprit, so obviously there is a place for these other forms of control too. The only sad thing is that quite a few foxes would have died unnecessarily, while attempts were made to catch the guilty party. On its own, the terrier is a very handy tool for the taking of foxes, for they will bolt them into nets, or will corner them deep inside the earth and remain with their quarry until dug out. Also, they are very useful for bolting foxes to waiting guns. But it has to be said that the lurcher/terrier combination is incredibly lethal

Beck emerging from the cellars under mill ruins where foxes often lie-up.

when it comes to the hunting of foxes and this method is popular, not only throughout Britain and Ireland (until the recent ban, that is!) but also in America and Australia. Terriers are used extensively throughout Europe too, especially in France, together with guns, hounds and lurchers, and many foxes can be taken using such methods.

Not that taking foxes with terriers, lurchers, or guns is easy, far from it, in fact. But it is true that these methods can very often result in more foxes being killed than is the case when using hounds. This is especially true when using a combination of lamp and lurcher. Lamping foxes at night and running them with lurchers can be a very effective form of control and one that is widely used in quite a number of different countries. Fox calls are used in order to bring the quarry within range and then the lurcher, or maybe a brace of lurchers, is slipped. Some may think this rather unsporting, but it is necessary to call foxes in as close as possible simply because they are masters at the art of escape and can easily slip through a hedge, or under a wall, or into an earth, before the lurcher has the chance to strike. Without calling foxes in to waiting lurchers, one would catch very few and control would be rendered ineffective to say the least. Do not forget, we are talking here about effective and efficient fox control, not 'sport', though I can assure the reader that this form of pest control is very exciting and full of fast-paced action.

Using lurchers

It is true that Reynard is very quickly and easily run down by a lurcher, when caught out in the middle of a reasonably large field, but that does not mean that a fox is easily caught. Reynard can turn on a sixpence, so to speak, and I have seen him turn a lurcher far more times than does a hare, and still manage to get away, despite the lurcher having a good long run at its quarry. Not that the dog was in any way at fault, for it was a notoriously good fox catcher, but it was simply because the fox is a wily beast that can often survive even when all the odds are stacked against it.

I personally have found that the very best fox catching lurchers are those with either Bedlington, Border collie, German shepherd dog, or Bull terrier blood in their make-up. A lad who hunts the

Pennine area of Lancashire has a GSD blooded lurcher and it is lethal with foxes, marking earths and catching them when either bolted with terriers, flushed from cover, or called in on the lamp. Bull terrier blooded lurchers are notorious fox killers and are used by many pest controllers. The Bull terrier blood gives them great power and a temper to match and they can be lethal fox catching dogs. Also, when socialised well in a family environment and walked on the street from being a puppy where other dogs are met, they can be incredibly good natured and only get 'fired up' whilst at their work. Bedlington terriers have a long history of working foxes and they have been used for creating excellent working lurchers for the past few centuries, lurchers that could take rabbits with fine agility, or run hares down with a combination of speed and sheer determination. Also, they would be powerful and game enough to tackle fox and were often used as seizure dogs at the end of badger digs. Derek Webster's lurcher, Rocky, is a Bedlington lurcher and it would be hard to find a better fox dog. I would say the vast majority of Bedlington blooded lurchers, if entered when the dog is mentally mature enough, make excellent fox catching dogs. The Border collie is not only intelligent and the very epitome of stamina, but it is also a very courageous breed that will guard the flock from both thief and predator. Whilst working

Lurchers are useful fox-catching dogs.

flocks out in the countryside, farm collies will sometimes come across foxes and most will give chase and kill a fox if they can catch it. On many occasions throughout the years, especially in places such as the Lake District, collies have disturbed foxes out on the fells and either given chase and seen them off, or caught and killed them.

The winter of 1885 was a very hard one indeed and the fells lay frozen for weeks at a time. John Thompson, a shepherd who raised sheep in the Borrowdale valley at the time, went out to gather in some sheep that he felt would be safer among the pastures of the lower dales, and certainly easier to tend with winter feed etc. Jim, his collie, obviously went with him and the dog soon located his flock and began bringing them down off the fells. However, the collie was distracted by a strong scent and the shepherd knew it would either be fox, or polecat. Jim hunted around a crag and then checked a borran, with a fox quickly bolting out of the rocks. The place must only have been shallow for this to happen. The collie, being of slight build and almost as nimble as a Whippet, gave chase and made good ground on its foe. What then followed was a long run that took the collie out onto the frozen fell tops and past crags and borrans where Reynard failed to get to ground, eventually being caught and killed below a crag. This event can be multiplied many times over, for collies make great fox killing dogs and they put this ability into lurchers bred by them. David Hancock's collie bred lurchers are a prime example of this, as these, generally, make great fox hunting dogs.

My own lurcher, Merle, had quite a bit of Bull terrier blood in his make-up and this, I am sure, gave him the edge when it came to working foxes. He wasn't a large dog, but was very powerful and could shake a fox like a terrier shakes a rat, quickly disorientating and killing his quarry. He also had a superb nose and this, together with his hound-like ears, betrayed the fact of either Beagle, or Foxhound blood, also being present. One of the most memorable hunts with Merle was when we had hunted several areas in the Western Pennines after shifting a few foxes for the local shepherds.

We had been busy controlling fox numbers throughout that springtime and lambing calls had virtually come to an end. This was our last day of the season and we were out on high ground on that early May morning, the sun soon warming us as it rose into a clearing sky, the thin cloud being slowly evaporated by the strengthening sunshine. We hunted through dense woodland and then emerged onto the rushy pastures of the valley, with the smooth sides of the hills rising into the sky all around, the grey of the stone piles and the crags clearly visible as the sunlight struck them. Earths are few and far between in this area and so Merle, Bess and Laddie, a Bedlington bred lurcher, hunted through the rushes as we headed deeper into the steep valley.

The terriers checked a long drain which runs across the fields until it reaches the brook below, but no foxes were residing there, nor had they been of late, for they showed no interest at all and quickly moved on. We now climbed the steep hillside and eventually reached the huge crag earth we had been heading for. Bella, a Jack Russell, was loosed from her couples and she entered the earth, exploring it eagerly. Although there proved to be no fox at home, there obviously had been recently, for the place was full of scent, which had enticed the experienced bitch below in the first place. The Russell emerged soon after, fully satisfied that the place was vacant, and so she was placed back on the couples while Pep and Judy were allowed to hunt around.

There is a long line of crags and rockpiles along the crest of this hill and we began making our way along while the lurchers and terriers continually checked for the presence of any skulking fox. About halfway along, the two loose terriers showed interest at a small rockpile and entered, quickly bolting a fox, which came out at the top and climbed up a narrow channel in the crag, finally reaching the top and disappearing out onto the moor above. Merle must have caught a glimpse of his foe just before it went from view, for he then scrambled over the rocks and began climbing the same route that fox had taken, only with not as much expertise! The going was far from easy, but at last he made it, with myself not far behind. Reynard had quickly disappeared by the time Merle had managed to reach open moorland, but its trail was quickly picked up and the lurcher was away, now hunting its line in fine Foxhound fashion. The scent was strong at first as I followed, with Merle sweeping to the left as the scent drifted on the warm breeze, but I could tell it wasn't going to last long, for the sunlight beamed down right onto this exposed moor and scent was very quickly fading. Merle hunted it as far as he possibly could and I am certain that, if scenting conditions were better, he would have located his foe and probably accounted for it. As it was, a May fox, by using cunning and the most likely way of successful escape, managed to secure its brush. Even though that fox escaped, it was a satisfying end to an eventful season, for the terriers had worked wonderfully well and the fox had given Merle a challenging hunt that was never going to succeed on a warm spring morning. And that, for me, is one of the things that makes fox control with hounds, terriers and lurchers, one of the most exciting and satisfying of all country pursuits, for the day is always totally unpredictable and the quarry is usually far more likely to escape than be caught, which makes hunting foxes very challenging indeed. Catching foxes against the odds, and very often seeing them escape while using a variety of crafty methods, is very rewarding, to say the least.

Some keepered spots are more difficult than others to work. Some gamekeepers will only allow the terriers to be kept on couples and lurchers must also be kept at close quarters, which means that one has no choice but to travel around the estate checking earths all day. Others will allow you to run the dogs loose, so that bushing foxes, as well as earth work, is then on the cards, which offers far more opportunities for effective control. Of course, during the shooting season, one is unlikely to be allowed to do anything but check earths, with the terriers coupled and the lurchers confined on their slip, but that is all one is allowed to do in some places, at any time of year.

Derek Webster hunts a couple of estates and the main work he has to do is to travel round the large estate with the keeper and check earths for occupation. If one is occupied, a terrier is entered and the fox bolted to the gun, or lurcher, or dug if it will not, or cannot, bolt. He has had some exciting hunts on these estates over the years and has caught a variety of foxes. Rocky, his lurcher, is a true marker of earths and, if he says an earth is occupied, then a terrier is entered in the sure knowledge that Reynard is indeed at home. At one spot, Rocky marked keenly and a terrier was entered. The fox soon bolted and was either shot, or Rocky took it. That fox was pure red in the main, but its back end and its brush were white; a most unusual coloration. At another spot, Rocky again marked and a terrier was put to ground. The fox would not, or could not, bolt, and so digging commenced. The soil is mainly light and slightly sandy on this estate and so the going was incredibly easy. The terrier was soon reached and a fox with just three legs was accounted for. How this fox had survived, or exactly how it had overcome its injury, I do not know, but my guess is that someone took the injured fox in and nursed it back to health and then it escaped, possibly digging its way out of the structure that imprisoned it. When folk take in injured, or young foxes, they do not realise just how hard it is to keep them confined and most will escape at some point.

The cunning of foxes was displayed when Derek was out with Barry Wild and Billy Fletcher, hunting farmland in Derbyshire that was owned by a Mr Bunting. There were few earths on this place, but still, there was a decent four-holed den that was worth checking

George Norman with his fox-catching lurchers.

115

out and when they got there a dead fox lay in the entrance to one of the holes. Gyp, Billy's terrier, went sniffing around the fox and then suddenly jumped over it and disappeared into the earth, where he began baying at a second fox, only this one was alive. Was that fox attempting to mask its presence with the scent of the dead one outside? I think it likely. However, the ploy failed. The hole came to a dead-end and they dug to Gyp who had killed a fully grown, but small, fox, by the time they reached him.

Lurchers that are used for the hunting of foxes must be courageous if they are to succeed in this form of pest control. Derek was out one night with a friend of his and they picked up a fox in the beam of the lamp. It was well within range and Derek told his hunting companion to slip his lurcher. 'I 'ave done', came the reply and Derek swung round in time to see the dog running away in the opposite direction! Not all lurchers are cut out to be fox dogs, for some simply will not enter to this quarry. Those that do, though, are a very effective tool when it comes to controlling foxes and they are most useful when used in conjunction with calls and the lamp. Derek was out lamping one night when two foxes were picked up in the beam. The brace of lurchers had seen their quarry and pulled eagerly at their slips, which were released immediately. The pair of running dogs then followed as the two foxes went over the brow of a hill and bedlam then broke out. Derek and his companion ran to the scene, only to discover that the dogs had come across a badger while coursing the two foxes, and their attention had quickly changed to 'Brock', who was now busily fighting off the two dogs. His companion panicked, shouting that the police would catch them and arrest them for hunting badgers, and, at that moment, a vehicle came up the farm track and the headlights poured all around them, lighting up the scene, as if in fulfillment of his prophecy. The panicking would-be foxhunter then put his arms up in the air, as though guns were fixed on him. It was an amusing sight for Derek and the owner of the vehicle, who, as it turned out, was only the farmer! The two lurchers were quickly pulled off the badger and 'Billy' simply ambled off and continued on his way, none the worse.

When hunting foxes with lurchers, one can use several methods. Flushing foxes from cover, or bolting them from earths, using terriers, is one way of doing it, or one could use small hounds maybe, such as teckels, or Beagle crosses, for bushing. Lamping foxes by calling them in is another method, and one that is incredibly effective, but there are other ways, though these can be far less effective than other methods already discussed. Simply waiting for foxes along a well used run, or close to a farmyard, is one way of dealing with a problem fox, though sometimes one can wait in vain. I remember spending an uncomfortable night waiting for a fox to turn up at an allotment where turkeys, reared in readiness for the coming festive season, were being taken regularly, despite the owner's best efforts to keep them out. That fox never appeared and it would have been far more effective to have gone lamping around those fields instead, though, of course, the guilty fox may not have been accounted for had I used this method instead and I hate to kill a number of innocent ones while attempting to catch the actual problem fox.

Hunting foxes in the traditional manner, using hounds, terriers and lurchers, is a very effective form of pest control, though hunting with hounds is undoubtedly *the* most selective method of all, as we have seen in this chapter. This is mainly because the sick, the weak and the old fall victim far more easily than do healthy foxes, though this can also be true when using either terriers, or lurchers. One late October day a few years ago, I was out with my terrier, Ghyll, when he began showing interest at a covert of brambles and bracken, which had by this time turned to the russet colours of autumn. We had been hunting the low country and had checked out several earths, but without success. Ghyll was a superb terrier and I used him both above and below ground. He was a powerful terrier and could push through the densest coverts with few problems, which meant that he often got away close to his fox when it emerged from the undergrowth, intent on staying well ahead of him. This was demonstrated one day when he flushed a fox from a bramble bush and came out on its brush, chasing and then hunting it until he followed it to ground, where he killed and stayed with his quarry until I got him out seven hours later.

He now entered this covert and soon after a fox was flushed, with Ghyll not far behind. I saw it as it emerged not far from where I stood and began running through sparse patches of bracken, but it wasn't making good progress at all. It seemed to have some injury, possibly to its pelvis, or lower back, and it ran awkwardly to say the least, now struggling to get away as Ghyll came bearing down on it at speed. No terrier on earth can match a fox for speed, not a healthy one anyway, so there was obviously something drastically wrong with this one. Soon after, Ghyll caught it and pinned it by the throat under a tree. I was quickly on the scene and finished it instantly with a heavy blow to the head. That fox was rather on the thin side and was obviously struggling to catch food for itself. It was in very poor condition and my guess is that it had been hit by a car and was struggling to survive because of its injuries. Death was inevitable, I just speeded up the process and saved that poor creature from a lot of suffering. The ban in England, Wales and Scotland, now makes it illegal to take foxes in this way and so many will suffer long lingering deaths as a result! For those countries where this activity remains legal, it may well be worth highlighting that the hunting of foxes using hounds and other dog breeds, is a very effective way of dealing with sick and injured individuals.

CHAPTER FIVE

CONTROLLING FOX NUMBERS WITHIN THE LAW IN ENGLAND, WALES AND SCOTLAND

AFTER a hard struggle to keep going, hunting with dogs in England and Wales, as I am sure you are very well aware, has now been banned and never has a more unjust, ignorant and prejudiced law reached the statute books! Also, before this, a law was passed in Scotland that also banned the hunting of foxes and other creatures such as mink, though these animals can still be flushed, as long as they are dispatched using a gun. The same is true in England and Wales; foxes can still be flushed to waiting guns, though not by large packs. Obviously, when one looks at this law, it is designed to prevent what are seen as 'toffs' from following hounds on horseback. It has nothing to do with animal welfare and everything to do with getting at the 'upper classes'. The problem is, it has affected the 'working classes' far more than anyone else!

Of course, there are sincere people out there who have fought for a ban on grounds that they thought were to do with animal welfare and certain practices within the hunting community have succeeded in producing enemies who, in the end, have succeeded in getting traditional hunting banned. Cub-hunting was one of *the* most emotive of all hunting practices and whoever thought of this term for the beginning of a new season wasn't thinking clearly at all, for the public immediately think of cuddly little fox cubs and imagine them being torn to pieces by large packs of savage hounds. What the public do not realise is that this form of hunting not only teaches young hounds how to conduct themselves in the field and

Terriers can still be used to ground in England Wales and Scotland, but they must be worked within the law.

how to hunt a scent, but it also disperses fox families that may otherwise hunt in packs and cause a great deal of loss to farm livestock if left unchecked. These young foxes are fully-grown by this time, if not fully fleshed out, and are wily beasts which quickly learn to avoid hounds at all costs. Again, as was discussed earlier, hounds are simply fulfilling the role of wolves, which would hunt down foxes that competed for food in their territory. And so cubhunting should have been known as 'dispersal' and thus less ammunition would have been given to opponents of hunting as a result. Politicians know that public image spells either disaster, or a successful career, depending on how they are viewed. It is a pity that the hunting world could not have learnt to be just as meticulous in this regard, for hunting may have been saved had the public image been improved years ago! Changing the term 'cub-hunting' to 'autumn-hunting' recently was far too little, far too late!

Stubbornly hanging on to tradition has cost the hunting world dearly and now they are being forced to change completely, no longer being allowed to hunt foxes in the traditional manner. However, it is still legal to kill foxes. The issue has never been about whether or not foxes should be hunted at all, but *how* they should be hunted. There is no question that foxes are agricultural pests and the evidence is overwhelming in support of their numbers needing to be controlled. Take the Second World War years as an example; a time when hunting with hounds was suspended. In time, the fox population swelled dramatically and fox shoots had to be organised up and down the country as farmers were reporting losses of livestock on a large scale, including lambs, chickens, ducks, geese, piglets and some even reported that packs of foxes were attacking calves. This makes much sense, for where they are not hunted by hounds, foxes pack. If coverts are disturbed on a fairly regular basis, a few times each season, and earths are also worked using terriers, then foxes will not gather in packs and they are less troublesome as a result.

Take hounds out of the picture, just as wolves were taken out of the picture due to the meddling of mankind, and problems will intensify, unless, of course, other measures of control are implemented. Large numbers of foxes, more than a score in some cases, were shot in just one day and it took quite a few years to bring the population back to reasonable levels. The same was true during the foot and mouth outbreak. The fox population swelled dramatically and farmers up and down the country suffered losses to their stock that they could ill-afford. So foxes need controlling, that is a fact that no amount of opposition can change. The only trouble is, in England, Wales and Scotland, this control, unless the ban can be overturned in court, can no longer be carried out using packs of hounds. This is sad, but I say to the hunts do not give up. Adapt your hunting and carry on as best you can, for if hunts give up, then its opponents have won the war. We will discuss ways of carrying on, regardless of the new law, and of how to keep within this law, while still carrying out effective pest control for farmers in each individual hunt country.

While Beagle packs can carry on by switching to rabbits and mink hunting packs to rats, fox hunting packs can no longer engage in this activity. Although hunting a fox and killing it with hounds is illegal in Scotland, in that country a pack can still be used to flush foxes to guns. In England and Wales, however, a pack cannot be used in this capacity. No more than two dogs can now be used to flush foxes and the animal must be dispatched using guns. There are other options available, though, and I believe it is possible to continue enjoying hound work and our glorious countryside, despite the ban. Hound trailing is one of these options and, with a little ingenuity and imagination, could be made into an exciting day out. This is possible if a hunt attempts to simulate a normal hunting day.

One of the most exciting events of a hunting day is drawing for quarry, when one keenly anticipates a find as hounds look for their fox, checking every covert carefully, with sterns moving from side to side continually, their nostrils twitching as they test for scent at

Like mounted packs, the fell packs must find a way to keep going until the ban is repealed, or a licensing system is hopefully introduced. (Blencathra Foxhounds '92)

every place. This could be simulated by the trail layer not telling the Huntsman exactly where it has been laid, or the direction it will take. He could give the Huntsman a rough idea of the area, but only enough information so that drawing is still necessary. Once the hounds pick up the line, then the hunt begins and the trail should be laid for some distance before being lifted in order that a check is simulated. One of the complaints about trail hunting is that hounds do not 'speak' to the line as eagerly as they do to live quarry, but in time the music of the pack should begin to improve, as they adapt to a new form of hunting. Most hunts are using a fox-based scent and mixed success has been the result. But with persistence things should improve until a good hunt can be enjoyed.

Where a check occurs, the Huntsman will then use his skill by taking hounds on and casting in the area where he believes the fox will have headed. This can be simulated in trail hunting too and one check, or several, can be put in place, but, again, the Huntsman and field should not be informed, so that the anticipation and excitement of making a cast can still be enjoyed. Also, with a little experimentation, a strong scent can be laid when the pace is required to be fast, a 'screaming' scent, or a weaker scent can be laid to simulate a cold drag, when hounds have to work out an old scent until they find and unkennel their quarry. At the end of the drag, which can be as short, or as long as one wishes, the kill can be simulated by scattering biscuits for the pack to enjoy as their reward.

In time, with persistence, trial and error, hound trailing could be fashioned to simulate a real day's hunting until, with refining and a little imagination, it near-resembles the real thing. Just as hounds adapted when changed from deer to fox, so will hounds adapt to this new form of hunting. True, there is nothing more exciting than searching for and hunting a fox on its terms, in its own environment, but isn't it also true that lovers of hunting go out, not for the sake of killing animals (though controlling fox numbers is important in any hunt country), but for the sake of enjoying the fresh air, stunning countryside and superb hound work, as well as, for the mounted field anyway, an exciting ride on horseback. All of these things can still be enjoyed if hound trailing is conducted as closely as possible to the real thing. Hunting folk are more than a little resourceful and I am certain they will make a success of trail hunting. With determination and backbone, every hunt in the country can continue and a season with hounds can still be rewarding. One of the benefits of hound trailing is that roads can be completely avoided. However, there is a danger that a fox will sometimes be found and hunted instead, but, if that was not the intention, then a prosecution would be very unlikely, for accidental hunting, we have been informed, will not result in legal action, providing there was no intention. If a trail has been laid, and this could be put on video at the start of each day as the scent is laid, as proof, then a defence could easily be made that hunting live quarry was completely unintentional.

The legal challenge to this ban, at the time of writing, is continuing, but it is impossible to say how successful it will be. Although pro-hunters have been told they have a good case, this challenge is incredibly expensive and we must face the possibility of failure. I sincerely hope that this ban is repealed, or amendments are made that would licence hunting, but success in this regard is not guaranteed. So it is no use hunting folk burying their heads in the sand and hoping they will be back to normal operations shortly. It could take a good few years to get this law repealed, or at least for amendments to be made that will allow licensed hunting, or all challenges could fail, so plans need to be implemented now, in order to keep hounds hunting, so that support does not dwindle in the future.

These plans should, I believe, include trail hunting which can, with imagination and resource, be made to simulate real hunting as closely as possible, along with a fox control programme for each area. It has been suggested that hounds could be used for flushing to guns by giving pairs to several followers, who would all be trained by, and be under the control of, the Huntsman and Whipper-in, all heading out and trying separate coverts with these pairs of hounds. True, this would provide work for many hounds, but think of all the foxes that would perish if several pairs of hounds were flushing foxes to guns at several different coverts. This form of hunting would wipe out the fox population in no time at all and is not, in my book, a viable option. True, one could miss many foxes and it would be impossible to prove that this was done purposefully, in order not to kill too many and severely deplete, or even wipe out, foxes in that hunt country, but that would risk

Wensleydale Foxhounds in kennel. Hunts must carry on as best they can, despite the ban in England, Wales and Scotland.

hounds getting away on a fox and several pairs being used in this manner would quickly form as a pack, which would then bring a risk of prosecution. True, if hunting occurs accidentally, without any intention of hunting in this manner, then legal action is unlikely to be taken, but still, this form of fox control has many disadvantages and will not, I am sure, suit most packs.

A pack of foxhounds could hunt a trail scent two days a week throughout the season keeping several couple of hounds for this

125

type of hunting alone. Besides these, a few couple of hounds could be kept for the task of flushing foxes to guns for up to four days a week, depending on the size of the hunt country of course. This would provide both enjoyable days out riding to hounds, as well as providing a fox control service to farmers and gamekeepers within each hunt country. This, I believe, would keep hunts going until the ban is repealed or amended, or, if the legal challenges should fail and the worst happens, at least hounds can continue to be hunted. If a trail is left without the exact whereabouts being given to the Huntsman and checks are included, so that the field can catch up and have a short rest, as happens when hunting live quarry, and so that the Huntsman can still make a cast, then I believe, with perseverance and time, a good day's hunting will still be enjoyed. Of course, this will not be as exciting as hunting live quarry, but still, with the Huntsman and followers having no idea of the way in which the trail will lead them, or for how long, the anticipation and excitement would still be enjoyed to some degree.

The English Lake District has a long association of hunting with hounds and it would be very sad if the fell packs gave up because of this ban. Like shire packs, fell packs must carry on regardless and keep hounds hunting. They could operate in a very similar way

A terrier sniffing at a well used couch in the undergrowth where foxes have been resting. A brace of dogs can be used to flush foxes to waiting guns.

to shire packs. They could have several couples hunting trails that could be as long, or as short, as followers wish. The Lakes has a strong car following and trails could be left so that hounds are in view of roads for much of the time. Again, checks should be included in the trail, so that the independent spirit is maintained, and the Huntsman given only a rough idea of the area of the start of the trail, so that he can draw with some degree of anticipation, and the route which it will take. He should follow as best he can on foot, as happens with live quarry, and help out if they cannot find the line at a check. At the foot of crags, the scent can be lifted and then laid again at the top, to simulate a fox going out onto open fell again, after losing them at such a rocky outcrop. This will keep hounds working in a similar way and will keep the action exciting for the followers. Of course, a fox is likely to be flushed on occasion and then hunted, but, again, this is not the fault of the Huntsman. The intention is to hunt trail and, again, the laying of the trail can be put on video at the start as proof, with the date and time on the display, just in case any investigation occurs.

This trail hunting could be carried out two days a week to keep a decent following and for other days of the week, the number depending on the size of the hunt country, the fell Huntsman and Whipper-in, along with any keen followers to assist, could then take a few hounds around different locations, using two at a time, of course, in order to flush and shoot foxes for farmers and keepers in that area. The keepered spots would also keep the terriers working. I know this is no perfect solution, but surely it is better than giving up. This positive action would keep hounds and terriers working (terriers can be used to ground on keepered ground and can be used to flush foxes to guns from undergrowth on any land where one has written permission) and would help maintain the social structure of the countryside. Hound breeding, though probably on a much smaller scale, will also continue and precious bloodlines will thus be preserved.

Many hunts will, I am sure, implement this sort of programme for keeping hounds hunting, even if it is an artificial scent, while at the same time providing a fox control service to local farmers and gamekeepers. Others may choose to implement hound exercise programmes, which would consist of long walks, with a mounted field, as well as foot and car followers, enjoying a day in the country. Of course, hounds are bound to pick up the scent of a fox and stopping them from hunting it, especially if it breaks cover close to them, would be very difficult indeed. In fact, after the ban came into effect on 18 February 2005, several foxes were killed by hounds. This has happened while both trailing and hound exercising and prosecutions have not come about simply because there were no intentions to hunt foxes during the day out with hounds. Indeed, even if there were intentions of hunting foxes, proving it in court would be very difficult, to say the least.

Although it is now illegal in England, Wales and Scotland, to hunt foxes using dogs, it is not illegal to use a pack of hounds, or any other breed of dog, to flush quarry for birds of prey. Any number of dogs can be used in this capacity and undoubtedly this will be one way in which some hunts can continue working a pack, though, again, they can only be used for flushing, not for hunting. In theory, as long as a hunt had someone out with any bird of prey on the fist, even a kestrel, then this would still be legal hunting, but it would be making a mockery of the law and would most certainly lead to these laws being tightened up. If packs do employ birds of prey, then the species used should be capable of taking foxes. Golden eagles take foxes in the wild, particularly fox cubs, though exactly how often foxes are preyed upon is difficult to say. Still, in the hands of a skilled falconer, Golden eagles would undoubtedly take adult foxes, but using them in conjunction with hounds would be very challenging indeed.

For one thing, the eagle must be broken to hounds so that it does not attack any of the pack members, should they come into close contact. Hounds must be so familiar with the eagle that they, in turn, if they were quickly on the scene of a successful catch, would not rush in and injure, or possibly kill, the eagle while trying to dispatch the fox. Also, because hounds are in covert, flushing quarry to a bird of prey, there must be a decent sized gap 'twixt the pack and the fox, before the bird could be released, in order to avoid any accidents. When a fox is flushed, there must be enough time for the eagle to catch its quarry and for the handler to quickly dispatch it, if the bird has not already done so, before the pack comes out of covert, intent on tasting their prey. This may mean allowing the fox to run on in order to flush it again, or simply trying for another instead. This then presents the danger of the pack getting away on the fox and hunting it. Flushing to birds of prey is not the simple answer it at first seems, that allows packs to continue working. This form of fox control must be planned carefully and advice must be sought from experienced handlers of birds of prey, for I am sure there are a number of falconers in Britain who already hunt foxes using eagles. If hunts paid a small fee for their services I am sure they would make a success of this form of hunting. Again, though, this method will not suit many, for hunting by scent remains illegal and flushing is all that hounds can do. With the trail hunting (fox-based)/fox control service combination, at least hounds get to work as they should.

Terriers can be used for flushing foxes to waiting guns in the same manner as can hounds, but, unless this is being carried out in order to prevent or reduce serious damage to game, or wild birds, which are kept, or preserved for the purpose of being shot, earth work is now forbidden under the new law. At the time of writing

A brace of terriers can still be used to flush foxes to waiting guns.

there are no clear guidelines exactly how this earth work can be conducted, but undoubtedly strict rules will soon be released by the Home Secretary. Rumours are rife and have included thoughts that a terrier will only be allowed to stay at a fox that will not bolt for any longer than twenty minutes, which would render digging impossible. Others have said that only baying terriers, and not fox killers, will be allowed to ground.

This is only speculation and we will have to wait and see. If only bolting foxes from earths is allowed, and not digging, then fox control would be very limited indeed using terriers to ground, for in many cases foxes just will not bolt. Also, in a tight stop-end, a fox will not be able to bolt because of being cornered by a determined terrier. A dig would then be required if the fox was to be accounted for. If there were a time limit set for a terrier to ground, then if that terrier could not be called out, the law would be broken once that time limit was exceeded. My terriers are very well behaved and, in the main, are obedient and easily controlled, but I cannot call them out once they are up to a fox. If they cannot reach their quarry, then after a little while, and more than a little shouting, I can call them out, but not so once they have reached their foe. So time limits would render earth work totally unworkable, if the fox refused, or could not, bolt. A few guidelines, however, are known, and it is appropriate to discuss them. The hunter of foxes must have written permission for either flushing foxes, or bolting them from earths. This permission should be carried with the hunter for it must be produced if requested by the police. Steps must be taken to ensure that the fox be bolted from below ground as soon as possible and that the fox is shot at the earliest opportunity. The terrier should be under close control in order that it does not prevent the fox from being shot. It is important that reasonable steps are taken to prevent injury to the dog, though this would be difficult if a fox chose to stay and make a fight of it. Only one terrier is to be used to ground at any one time. Earth stopping can still be practised, but not with regard to badger setts. Also, when, and if, a code of practice is issued by the Home Secretary, these rules must be adhered to. The National Working Terrier Federation, your local terrier club or The Countryside Alliance, will be able to keep you informed of such practices and of the best way of working terriers within the law.

The rules regarding the use of only one terrier to ground at any one time may seem to make the entering of youngsters rather difficult, but this is not necessarily so. True, it is easier to enter a novice by allowing it to see other terriers at work and to do a little work with them, but this ban and its silly and unnecessary rules will not prevent the entering of youngsters. Two terriers can be used to flush foxes from undergrowth to waiting guns, or for study and observation purposes (i.e. in order to ascertain the size of local populations, or to research which type of daytime retreat they favour), provided the hunter has written permission from the landowner, or he himself owns the land, and so a young terrier can be worked alongside an older, experienced terrier and much will be learned whilst bushing foxes. For one thing, fox scent will become very familiar to a young terrier and that will come in handy when you begin using it to ground.

Terriers, having roots that have sprung from ancient breeds of hounds such as Beagles, have incredibly sensitive noses and just by testing the entrance to an earth, if a novice has already bushed several foxes above ground, it will quickly tell you if the earth is occupied, or otherwise. The youngster will then be able to locate its quarry, for it will already have been finding foxes above ground, sometimes in undergrowth that is so dense, it is almost like working an earth. Bushing foxes to waiting guns can begin when the novice is about eight months of age, but earth work should not begin until at least twelve months, even later for more sensitive types. This means that a young entry will have had at least four months of experience above ground, before it begins earth work. This experience will enable it to enter more quickly and some work like veterans right from the start, especially if they are bred from good working bloodlines. Many terriers are self-entering anyway, especially those that come from a long line of workers, so make sure your stock, whatever breed you choose to use, is from proven working lines.

When bushing foxes, it is important not to enter at too early an age. Foxes, generally, will flee very quickly from terriers that enter covert, but there is always the chance that one may choose to stay and fight. This is quite rare, but does happen. This has happened to my terriers on several occasions, so this is more likely the more often one engages in this type of work, for my terriers have bushed

The author's wife with Fell terriers in a typical rough northern landscape. (West Yorkshire moors)

literally hundreds of foxes over the years, to lurchers, guns and for research purposes, and so they have encountered reluctant foxes on a number of occasions. One of the most memorable of these was one day when my brother and I were out with two of my terriers, Mist and Fell. Mist was far less experienced at the time and she was learning much by working alongside Fell, who had served two seasons at the Pennine Foxhounds and really knew his stuff.

We were drawing along a steep hillside above a wood and Fell and Mist showed keen interest as they rooted among the dense heather and dead stalks of bracken. They began baying and suddenly a fox leapt out of the undergrowth and ran down into the wood, with the terriers in hot pursuit. My brother and I quickly followed as the terriers hunted the scent through the wood and out onto a hillside covered in bracken, with two large gorse coverts close to the top. We stood at the bottom as Fell pressed on ahead and entered the gorse, where, unusually, the fox had stopped running. It waited for Fell to catch up and the pair could be heard grappling inside the impenetrable undergrowth. The fox, though, broke away and came out of the gorse, running along the top of the hill for a few hundred yards and entering the second gorse covert, where, again, the fox waited and then began fighting with the terrier once more. Eventually, finding its opponent to be a little too fierce for it, the fox was flushed again and this time it got out of there rather rapidly, with Fell losing it a short time later. This is a most unusual occurrence, but foxes will sometimes stay and make a fight of it, if for only a minute or so, and so it is important not to use a terrier, even for bushing foxes, at too young an age, lest a bad bite put it off. By bushing foxes in this manner, a youngster will learn much that will aid it when it comes to starting earth work where reared birds, or wild birds, are kept and preserved for shooting.

Terrier work remains as normal in Scotland, but the quarry must be bolted and shot, or dug out and shot, and so there remains much scope for normal terrier work in this country. And digging foxes can be a very effective way of controlling fox numbers. Locators are necessary in this day and age, for the terrier can be more quickly located and dug out when using this type of equipment. I never could afford a locator when I first began working terriers. These devices were in the early stages of development back then and were rather unreliable anyway, but these days they are essential pieces of equipment and are, in the main, very reliable and accurate. New devices are now coming onto the market and these, hopefully, will improve the locating of terriers, though I cannot help but feel that the modern terrierman has missed out on a skill that was developed during those days prior to locators becoming available. Locating terriers deep inside an earth and then digging down virtually to the exact spot, was a skill developed by terriermen who did not have the luxury of locators and I am proud to say that I was one of those who developed this knack, skill, call it what you will, that is rarely seen nowadays. A dig I took part in during the early part of 2005 saw me having to rely on that knack I had developed before I began using locators and I was glad to find that I have not lost this skill (see chapter on urban foxes). Another dig I took part in a few years ago was another opportunity to use this skill. But before we discuss this dig, I would just like to warn those who bush foxes to make certain they know very well the area in which they are working.

This is essential because of both badger setts and fox earths. Even when rabbiting it is essential to know the country well, for accidents can happen if badger setts and fox earths are not located *before* beginning hunting an area. When I hunted a small pack of terriers and teckels a few years ago, along with John Hill, a couple of foxes were found and one of them accounted for. Of course, before the ban this would not have been an issue, but since 18 February 2005 one would be in breach of the law in this situation. The pack were hunting a dense growth of brambles which were spread over quite a large area. The main body of the pack flushed and chased a fox from the covert, but Fatima, a very small teckel bitch, was not seen, though we could hear her baying in what seemed like the far distance. We eventually located her inside a dug-out rabbit hole, baying strongly at her quarry, and Fell quickly joined her, though we managed to stop the rest from getting to ground. Fell managed to push past Fatima and then he quickly throttled his fox inside that earth. Had this occurred now, then we would run the risk of prosecution. So know your country well and avoid fox earths that cannot be worked due to the exemption rule not applying on land where game birds are not reared, or wild birds are not preserved for shooting. Of course, accidents will happen on occasion, but as long as there is no intent, then no prosecution should follow, although this has yet to be tested in court!

Once written permission has been gained to either flush foxes to guns, or to hunt rabbits, or even both, it is best to walk over that land during the winter and get to know it well. The undergrowth will be sparse during the winter months and earths and badger setts are more easily located at this time of year. Also, one can ask the farmer if he knows of any setts, or fox earths, in order that they can be avoided. Once done, the bushing of foxes, or bushing rabbits, or both, can begin. However, despite the greatest of care to remain within the law, as I have already stated, accidents can, and will, happen.

I was once out tracking foxes and just generally enjoying a day out in the snow-covered countryside. I had Rock with me and allowed her to run loose as I walked through a wood, the topsides of the bare branches covered in a layer of snow and the woodland floor carpeted to a few inches depth. Rock was busy bushing the few rabbits that remained above ground from sparse bramble thickets and I just let her get on with it while I searched for fox prints. The wind was icy cold and the sky laden with more snow-burdened clouds, but I forgot about the hostile conditions when I found plenty of fox tracks on the edge of this wood. I called for Rock to return to me, as I did not want her running all over the place and spoiling the tracks, but she failed to respond to my call.

I wasn't too worried though, for she had bushed and chased a couple of rabbits and was probably marking at a warren, so I was sure she would soon return, once she got a little fed up of digging. However, some time later I realised that she was not marking a rabbit hole and must have caught the scent of a fox and headed off in search of it. There is a massive covert which consists of incredibly dense brambles on the edge of this wood and I was sure she had headed into here, so I waited for her familiar bark that would signal a find and a flash of russet moving swiftly across the snow, which was often the scene that followed such a find. As the minutes passed by, I realised that I was wasting my time waiting for such occurences, for I was now sure she was to ground somewhere in that huge covert.

The only trouble was, as I circled the covert, listening all the while for a distant baying sound that would help me locate the area in which she had gone to ground (she had no locator collar on, for I had no intention of putting her to ground), along with Rock's prints, were human footsteps, so I began to worry that someone had picked her up. I carried on searching until darkness began to creep on, then headed off for help. Tim was an experienced terrier-man and I called on his help. We returned after dark, the snow aiding us to find our way, but there was not a sound to be heard, just the oppressive silence of the empty landscape all around. I feared my terrier had either been stolen, or had been picked up by someone mistakenly thinking she was lost, but I had not given up on the idea of her having got to ground, so I determined to return first thing in the morning, with digging tackle, and locate my bitch. I had never lost a terrier to ground and was not going to allow this to be the 'first time for everything'.

I was up early the next morning and, after putting digging equipment in the car, went to pick up my brother, Mike, who had volunteered his help. And then, in order to help locate my bitch, went to pick up Rock's daughter, Bella, who was at my mother's house. We arrived at the spot at about 9am and I took Bella to the massive covert. This undergrowth covers a vast area, growing profusely all over the hillside of a small valley, but I was sure that Bella could find her mother for me, though no doubt she would need to search the place for some time. I put a collar on her, with a bell attached, in order that I could follow her progress around the undergrowth, and then loosed her at the top of the covert, around the middle part of it.

She immediately headed off to the right and went straight to an earth close to the edge of the covert, where she began marking eagerly. Bella was a large terrier and the tunnel was a little tight, so she whimpered and barked as she dug, guiding my brother and me to the spot, which we reached after beating our way through the

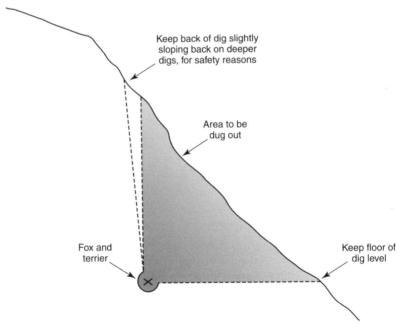

Digging foxes on steep hillside.

undergrowth. This was the middle of winter, but still, that undergrowth was very dense and difficult to get through. However, after a good beating with a stout walking stick, we managed to reach the spot and I was sure this was the earth where Rock had entered during the previous day's outing. I pulled Bella away, but could hear nothing. Despite this, though, I went to the car and fetched the digging tackle and operations began immediately.

Mike and I were down to our T-shirts in no time at all, for, despite the severe cold, we were sweating as we cleared the brambles from around that earth, cutting through the tough prickly stalks and flattening them, until we had a space we could work in. On flat ground, when digging to any great depth, it is best to cut a trench, which can include steps for deeper digs, after cutting squares of turf that should be replaced once the back-filling has been done (this is especially important on pasture), but this was a steep hillside, so one must cut into the hill, while all the time keeping the ground one is working on level (see diagrams). Rather

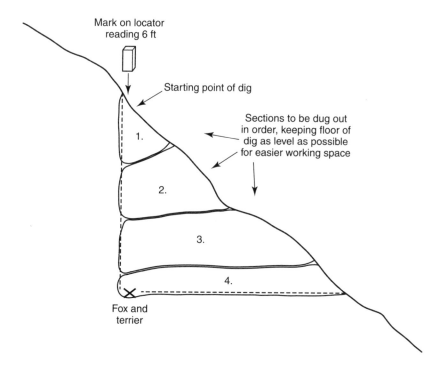

Mark on locator
reading 6 ft

Starting point of dig

Sections to be dug out
in order, keeping floor of
dig as level as possible
for easier working space

1.

2.

3.

4.

Fox and
terrier

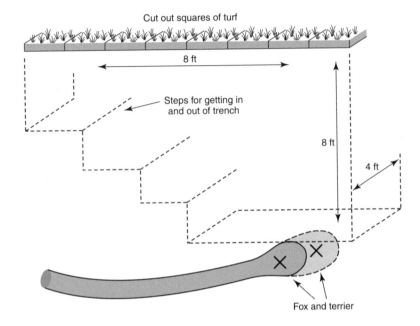

Cut out squares of turf

8 ft

Steps for getting in
and out of trench

8 ft

4 ft

Fox and terrier

Fox digging on pasture. (Sizes are approximate) Give yourself plenty of room to work.

than squares of turf, we had the rubbery roots of brambles to cut through and so the digging was very hard indeed. The spade bounced off the thicker roots and it took quite some time to clear them until, finally, we had softer ground to work with. Or so we thought. All kinds of rubbish was dug up as we made slow progress and stones, cinders, gravel, old bottles and bits of metal coming out of the ground as we dug ever deeper, trying all the time to keep the hole clear. I put a stick inside the hole and this ensured we did not lose and fill it in forever, which would have meant the death of the terrier from suffocation. We cut into that steep hillside still further, all the time making good progress, but the cinders falling back into the area already dug out made the going both difficult and slow.

The work continued and we made steady progress until, at last, we could hear the bitch a few feet away, whimpering, which told us she was stuck and could not make her own way out. Now absolutely certain of the location of Rock, this spurred us on and the last few feet was cleared rapidly, until we at last retrieved my

1.

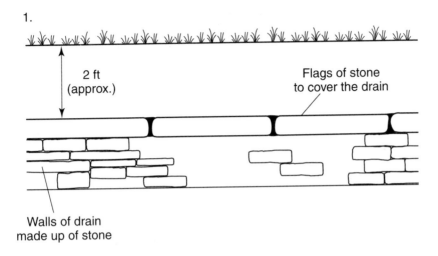

2 ft
(approx.)

Flags of stone
to cover the drain

Walls of drain
made up of stone

1. Dry-stone drain. These are approximately 18 inches to 2ft deep and often hold foxes.

2. By digging down and lifting flagstone, one can easily recover the terrier and fox.

Dig must leave enough room
to lift flag-stone

2.

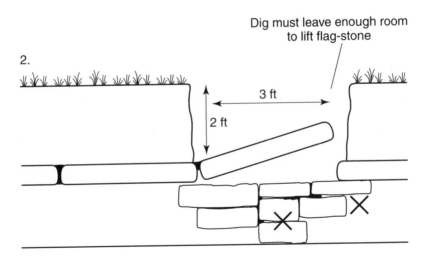

3 ft

2 ft

Terriers can still be used to flush foxes to guns, as long as written permission is granted on land where birds are reared, or preserved, for shooting.

bitch. She had been to ground for twenty-six hours by this time and had killed her fox in the tight stop-end. Because the hole was very tight, she had dug on to her quarry and the soil and cinders she had thrown behind her, had been preventing her from getting out. Bella had been invaluable in that rescue and I am certain I would not have found my terrier without her. The local paper published an item about the rescue, which was deemed rather unusual to say the least.

This is a good reason for knowing your country well, for terriers can simply disappear as if into thin air. One minute they are there, the next there is neither sight nor sound of them. If one does not know the country to be hunted, then there is a real danger of losing a terrier in this situation. Also, concentrating on exactly where your terriers are, when bushing, is important. A lapse in concentration can mean the loss of a terrier should it get to ground. I can proudly say that, despite having terriers trapped to ground on many occasions and having taken part in several rescues, I have never lost a terrier to ground, though Roy and I came very close to doing so, one day when we were hunting at the foot of the bleak Western Pennines.

Roy carried out repairs on farm machinery for a number of clients and one of them raised sheep in the shadow of the wind-swept hills close to Bolton in Lancashire. As you can imagine, he lost quite a number of lambs to foxes during each springtime and so we were asked to carry out control throughout the winter and spring months, which we were happy to do. He also kept quite a few chickens too, which, as well as being for the family table, were part of his livelihood. He was also a dairy farmer, as well as a shepherd, and he sold his freshly laid eggs to many of his clientele. So his fine laying hens were an important part of his means of living, not some hobby which had the benefit of putting fresh eggs on the table each morning.

We had been busy during the previous spring on this farm and had shifted a few foxes that had been causing problems up until around the middle of May, when lambing problems often end. After an enjoyable summer off-season, we were now back on this farm, carrying out a control programme that would hopefully keep lamb losses to a minimum when springtime came around once more. Roy kept a couple of terriers, as did I, along with a lurcher and an ex-track racing greyhound which was proving useful as a rabbiting and fox hunting dog. The small bobbery pack were loosed and they began hunting the pastures as the sun broke through the dense clouds, the dew sparkling as it clung to the grass stalks and the cobwebs scattered everywhere, illuminated by the sunlight, which highlighted the warm autumn shades of the leaves that would soon be shed, once the fierce autumn gales arrived.

The pack got busy with their noses to the ground and hunted across the dew-soaked pastures in search of scent, being diverted a little as the hot scent of moles working around their little hills caught their attention. Sometimes the terriers will pop their snouts into a mole-hill and pull out their prize, but usually the moles have long gone, leaving pastures, even golf courses, in rather a mess. The sweeping hills and the lower vales were clothed in glorious sunshine for a time, but then, a little later, the grey swirling mist came in and shrouded the hills in its density, blotting out the once familiar landscape of rich pasture broken only by the long, untidy lines of ancient and, in some places, tumbling, stone walls, the trees dotted about and the rising bulk of the menacing hills all around. Even though one knows a country well, once that mist comes in and blots out familiar landmarks, one could be anywhere and it is so easy to get lost in this situation.

The pack continued to work hard as we crossed the pastures, but a little later we noticed that one of the Jack Russell terriers was missing. Terriers are busy little hunting dogs and are notorious for disappearing on a hot scent, or even going to ground unnoticed, so it is important to be aware of their whereabouts at all times. This is why it is also important to know of every earth in the vicinity. The only trouble is, when there are several dogs hunting, or one strays onto land that isn't so well known, which is very easy to do when hunting on a very misty day, it is easy for a dog to slip away without being seen. The dense shroud enveloping that wild country meant that we did indeed stray onto unfamiliar ground and the terrier had slipped away without our noticing it. Despite our shouts for her to return, Judy was obviously not going to respond and so a search party would be necessary.

We set off in the direction of the area in which she had last been seen and we wandered over every field in the immediate vicinity, looking out for earths or rabbit burrows she may have dug into, and listening all the while for her strong, steady bay. Judy was a game little bitch and had a habit of finding previously unknown earths. Roy was once out walking on a snow-covered midwinter day when Judy suddenly disappeared. He heard her loud bay coming from a drain closeby and suddenly a fox, in fine condition with a magnificent winter coat, exploded from out of the ground as it bolted at speed from the yapping terrier close on its brush. He watched as it ran away, twisting and turning through the ancient trees of Redisher Wood, its russet coat standing out starkly against the white backdrop, the little terrier in hot, but vain, pursuit. On another occasion, Roy was out bird watching one hot summer day when he sat down on the hillside above Ramsbottom in Lancashire, intent on enjoying a pint of ice cold milk. Judy had once again done her disappearing act and Roy sat there looking around for her. All of a sudden a fox burst out of the ground, the long grasses having hidden the entrance and exit to a stone drain which runs along this hillside, and ran off down the hill, with a second, then a third, fox following, and Judy once again in hot, but vain, pursuit. Once again she had done her disappearing act and we were now certain she was to ground somewhere closeby.

Roy thought he could hear something nearby and he headed off to investigate, while the mist came in in even denser waves. I watched as the mist enshrouded him until, very soon, he was completely gone from view, the eerie silence descending now that I found myself alone. It was a strange sensation; standing there in that field with an impenetrable grey mist pressing in heavily upon me and with the sound of what seemed to be distant thunder, but getting rapidly closer. And then came the sound of what I was sure was a man running, but with much urgency in his steps, that sound of rumbling thunder growing louder and louder. I looked into the grey swirl with strained eyes and at last captured some form of movement from deep within. And then, now becoming ever clearer, was the form of Roy heading towards me, with blind panic stricken across his features, his face pale, his eyes sunken and fixed intently on the fence he was now approaching. And that is when all became suddenly clear.

It wasn't thunder at all. Coming racing out of the mist and getting ever nearer to the fleeing Roy, was a huge bull which hadn't been put off its course by the fact that it probably hadn't seen much of Roy until now, driven on in its rage by either the scent, or the sound, of the intruder who had so rudely stumbled into its territory. Roy had been transformed into something resembling an Olympic hurdler and so, just before that snorting belligerent bullock reached him and splattered him across the bleak autumn landscape, he jumped and cleared the fence with ease, in spite of the fact that it was high enough to keep horses in! Once he had managed to catch his breath, steadying himself after the shock and the exertion of it all, he told me that he had found Judy stuck inside a stone drain which, unfortunately, just happened to be in the same field as that raging bull. However, the drain, he said, was not far from the fence, so maybe we could sneak back into that field and dig her out without that snorting mound of death knowing much

143

about it. Had it caught up with him, that bull would certainly have made a mess of Roy, so we had no intentions of giving it another chance at either one of us. Gingerly, we climbed over the fence and made our way as quietly as possible to the drain and quickly located the little bitch. She had entered the drain and had obviously bolted a fox, but, somehow, had become trapped, probably due to breaks inside that prevented her from emerging. The fox, being slimmer and far more agile, having negotiated these breaks easily.

We didn't hang around. We cut a few squares of turf and then dug down a couple of feet through quite easy-going soil, until the spade hit the stone slab that had been placed over the sides of the drain. We then cleared all of the soil from off the top of the slab and lifted it, at last freeing the terrier. And then, after a quick backfill, we got out of there as quickly as possible, relieved that that bullock had remained clueless as to our whereabouts! Judy was none the worse and we were glad to have found her so quickly.

Experiences such as these quickly teach the hunter of foxes, as well as rabbits, to be aware of the earths in any area to be hunted. This is especially so now that certain practices have been banned in England and Wales in particular. Avoiding earths, of course, is not necessary on land where game birds are reared, or wild birds are preserved for shooting, when one has written permission to be working such land, but even then it is necessary to make certain that only one terrier gets to ground at any one time. Where one has written permission to bush foxes to guns, but that land is not used for rearing game birds, or wild birds are not preserved for shooting, then earth work is out of the question. The only trouble is, a fox could dig an earth during the night before a hunt is to take place and the terriers used for bushing could easily get to ground and either kill, bolt, or bottle up their fox in a stop-end.

I was recently out hunting rabbits and the terriers were busy bushing them. I was in an area where I have never known there to be fox earths, but there were plenty of rabbit burrows and the terriers marked quite a few. This population is recovering from bad outbreaks of myxomatosis and so I was not using a ferret, just allowing the dogs to give them a little exercise and excitement. At one spot, Mist and Turk disappeared into what had been a small rabbit warren. I was soon on the spot and was in time to prevent Beck from getting to ground too. I listened and the two terriers were baying strongly. A fox had dug into the rabbit hole, probably intent on making a kill, but had then decided to make the place its home. I had no way of knowing it was there and now found myself in breach of the law. The fox then bolted and the terriers were not far behind, emerging and speeding off on the hot scent. They hunted it through the wood and then down into the valley, where it eventually crossed the brook and headed out onto a very steep hillside full of shale, where, at long last, the terriers lost the scent. My terriers are very obedient and well behaved, but they will not be distracted from following a fresh scent by any amount of cries for their return. So remaining within the law is virtually impossible in this sort of situation, but one must make the effort to do so.

Terrier lads can still find work for their dogs by gaining permission for earth work on keepered estates and rough shoots, which are becoming ever more popular throughout the country, and by bushing foxes to waiting guns. Lurcher lads can use their dogs for bushing foxes too, as long as there are no more than two at a time. The danger with this, of course, is that the lurchers will catch their quarry, or be so close to it as to make shooting impossible. Also, when coverts are very dense, lurchers will struggle to work them and there is no substitute for terriers, or small hounds such as Bassets, or teckels, in such circumstances. Hunts can keep going by implementing a programme that includes trail hunting in a way that simulates real hunting as closely as possible, making certain that the laying of the trail is captured on video as proof of intent, just in case a fox is put up and mistakenly hunted. They can also practise fox control, flushing them using a couple of hounds and shooting them. Also, in order to keep a close eye on the fox population, making certain that it is not being decimated, a research programme could also be put into operation by hunts around the country, which could spend some time flushing foxes from covert and allowing them to escape unharmed, just to assess numbers in each hunt country. This could possibly be carried out throughout August, before hunting begins properly. There remain quite a few options open to hunts that will ensure they keep going, with financial support from followers of course, who can become fully involved in all of the different aspects of hunt activity. Giving up now would only justify the ignorant, prejudiced campaigns of those who know nothing of country matters. All must dig their heels in and carry on, striving to remain within the law, despite it being unworkable, unenforceable, unpractical and downright wrong!

I have just been reading about the intent of Australia's RSPCA to try to persuade the powers that be to follow Britain's shameful example in banning hunting with dogs, in order to 'improve' the welfare of the fox. What planet do these people come from? The fox in Australia has caused devastation among its small rodent populations and all methods of control, including with hounds, must remain an option in that country. Fox hunting with hounds, when carried out for the sake of control, and not 'sport', is a very effective tool indeed and, if hunts operate at full capacity, possibly using terriers and guns where necessary, will do much to reduce the fox population to reasonable levels. All countries where hunting with hounds is carried out, will find themselves having to fight for their way of life more and more in the future, for bans will be called for by growing numbers of opposers in these countries. Again, as mentioned earlier, it would be prudent of hunting associations to get together and look closely at practices that fuel opposition and try to work out some way in which these can be modified, or even done away with, in a manner that improves the welfare of the hunted fox, as well as the efficiency of control. Take the circling of coverts as an example.

So-called cub-hunting was once carried out by putting hounds into covert and then circling it, while the riders beat on their saddles and boots with their hunting whips in order to drive the young foxes back so that the young hounds had a better chance of being involved in a kill. I believe this practice was voluntarily stopped in more recent years, and rightly so. Young hounds will learn over the course of the first two seasons and such artificial entering methods are completely unnecessary. In the same manner, the hunting world should closely examine its practices and make improvements where it is deemed essential in the fight to preserve a future for hunting live quarry with hounds. It is pointless hanging on grimly to tradition and then losing everything anyway! In these times when the public image is especially important and dealing with quarry in a responsible way that really considers the welfare of the animal and not concentrating on 'how long can we keep the hunt going for?' will, I am sure, help to break down much ignorance and prejudice in a way that will keep hounds hunting in those countries where this practice remains legal.

As for the ban in England, Wales and Scotland, well, it appears that those bans are here to stay, particularly in Scotland. In this country, though, many more foxes are being accounted for by hunts because, at one time, hounds would have flushed maybe five or six foxes from covert and only one, two at the most, if the pack split, were in danger of being caught. Now, with marksmen shooting those foxes that are flushed, in order to satisfy the law, all five or six foxes are usually shot. And these laws are supposed to be about animal welfare! In England and Wales, as time goes by, that incredibly unworkable law will be shown to be so more and more and possibly changes will be made. Let us hope that legal challenges will succeed, but we cannot count on that. The best hope is for concessions to be made and for some sort of licencing to be introduced.

For example, if a fox is shot and wounded, then the law should allow a pack to hunt and account for that wounded animal, to avoid what will be a long, lingering death from starvation, or infection. In the hilly country, especially where there are large tracts of forestry, packs should be allowed to hunt these areas, for it is the best way of dealing with foxes in that type of country. Two hounds will not succeed in flushing foxes from forestry. A pack has difficulty in doing this, so two hounds would be useless in such a situation. Also, when chickens, lambs, or piglets are being preyed upon, hounds (and, indeed, terriers) should be allowed to be called in and the scent of the guilty fox picked up and hunted until, hopefully, it is accounted for and its crimes ended, not for the sake of 'sport', but for the sake of the livelihood of the farmer.

Instead of two hounds, a pack should be used for flushing foxes from larger coverts and the guns should be allowed to use their discretion. If a number of foxes have been shot from one covert and others continue to be flushed, then the gun should be able to allow some to run on, in order to prevent a population from being decimated, if he feels it necessary. And if the pack then get away on one of those foxes, the law should allow for this possibility. Nobody, I am sure, would object to a common sense law that really does have the welfare of the fox in mind, while at the same time allowing for efficient control which would include the use of packs

147

of hounds. For example, if the law had stated that hounds could still be used to hunt foxes, but that the quarry must be dealt with as soon as possible, either shooting a fox as it left covert, provided a safe shot was possible, catching it with hounds as quickly as possible, or running it to ground and digging it out and shooting it, then I am certain this would have been more palatable. This would end any inclination to make hunts last for as long as possible and thus would improve the welfare of a hunted animal and the efficiency of control. Also, because shooting, or digging out, would not be a dictated end to a hunt, foxes would still have the opportunity of getting away unharmed. This would ensure that selective control continues and a healthy population is maintained. The ban in England and Wales could have two different effects, depending on which way things go.

If, for example, flushing and shooting is carried out extensively, the risk is that so many foxes will be accounted for that they become a rarity in our countryside, as was the case in many areas of the country during earlier centuries when foxes were hunted down without mercy. Or, if control isn't carried out effectively in many areas, due to folk giving up altogether because of this law, then the population could swell so dramatically that farmers (not to mention wild birds) suffer even more severe problems with fox predation. Also, distemper and mange would proliferate and far more foxes will suffer in this sort of situation. And, where there are sick foxes, there are far more problems with livestock losses. Sick foxes will always prey upon the more vulnerable and so lambs and poultry, as well as other livestock kept around a farmyard, will always be at risk from a weak predator which, after all, will be unable to catch anything else but a few insects. The use of hounds, terriers, or lurchers, has always been a very effective way of removing sick and injured foxes from areas where livestock is vulnerable to attack. However, now that the shooting of foxes is the only option available in England, Wales and Scotland, along with trapping and snaring of course, far more healthy foxes will perish along with the sick, the weak and the old!

Whilst digging with terriers one always had the option of allowing the quarry to run for another day. If a fox full of mange was dug, or one with injuries, or it was old, or sick, then, of course, one would put the poor beast out of its misery, if the terrier hadn't already done so. But sometimes a terrierman may deem it necessary to allow the fox to live, once the dig is complete. This is especially true in areas where the lamping of foxes is carried out on a fairly regular basis. Calling foxes in and shooting them is a very effective means of control and large numbers can be taken. If one is on land rabbiting and a terrier goes to ground on a fox, one would now be breaking the law, but before this law was passed one would simply dig the terrier out and either finish the fox, or let it go, in order to allow existing stocks to replenish depleted numbers a little. Now, with this new law in force, one is obligated to shoot any foxes that are flushed, bolted, or dug out. I have released foxes on quite a few occasions at the end of a dig, for reasons already discussed, which was always done for the welfare of the fox population, if numbers were getting too low (assessing numbers in an area can easily be done by working coverts and earths), but that option is no longer available to the terrierman. We have passed from a self-regulating practice based on discretion, to a kill, kill, kill policy that has the full might of the law behind it. This is what happens when the ignorant and prejudiced interfere in affairs they know nothing about!

CHAPTER SIX

TRAPPING AND SNARING

LAMBS are being taken regularly from pastures that border land where the hunter of foxes has no permission to go, very often because the landowner is a lover of foxes and is completely against any form of control. The farmer may be suffering from poultry, duck, or geese losses, or maybe a combination of these. So what can be done in order to put an end to this threat to a stockman's livelihood? The foxes in question could be shot, either using a call and a lamp, or by waiting for the culprits to approach the farm using favourite runs through the fields and hedges, or, alternatively, one could trap, or snare them.

Foxes will live on motorway verges, railway embankments and often in quarries, even ones still being worked, and in such locations it is impossible to deal with them effectively, hence the need for trapping, snaring or shooting, a subject we will deal with in detail a little later. If the landowner is anti-hunting and will not allow anyone on in order to deal with foxes taking livestock, then trapping and snaring may be the only option available to the farmer suffering losses to his livestock. A farmer I was carrying out pest control for had suffered quite a lot of livestock losses and one winter's day I was on his land, intent on reducing fox numbers. I had Rock and Ghyll with me, two first rate working Fell terriers, and I had walked around the fields and out onto the moorland in order to check all of the earths in that area, but all to no avail. There had been quite a heavy fall of snow during the night and so it wasn't long before I came across fresh fox tracks that I was easily able to follow.

I kept the terriers on couples by my side in order to prevent them from spoiling the trail and just walked along the tracks for quite some distance, until they led onto the top of a nearby quarry. I then continued following the twisting and turning trail all over the quarry until, finally, I was able to go no further. The tracks led right into the yard where the stone products were stored in readiness for transporting to customers and the foxes, two of them, probably a courting couple, must have been laid up somewhere among these products, or possibly under one of the buildings that were used as offices etc. I could do nothing about this situation, though, for I had no permission to hunt the place and the workers regularly fed the local fox population during the evening, enjoying watching them as they fed under the huge lamps that light up the quarry at night. So there are times when hunting with dogs is completely ineffective and other methods must be employed. In this situation, the snare and trap come in very handy indeed.

Trapping

Live traps are very effective for catching foxes that are making a nuisance of themselves, but this form of fox control must be carried out in a humane way. One often hears tales of terrier lads catching foxes in live traps and taking them to an artificial earth where they are put inside in order for young terriers to be entered in this way. These tales, in a few rare cases, are undoubtedly true, but most decent terrier lads would not even dream of using such artificial methods of entering, methods, which, in the main, do little for young terriers anyway. A fox in a truly wild state is the only really effective way of entering a novice terrier and no other way will do. Besides, such methods are incredibly cruel and foxes will suffer great stress in this sort of situation. Methods such as this will always be used by a few of the working terrier brigade, no matter what the law says, so if bans are brought in because of such practices, then those bans will fail miserably. Hunting folk who truly have respect for their quarry will always avoid and abhor such unnecessary practices. Of course, the hunting ban in England and Wales in particular, could tempt many terrier lads to use this form of artificial entering from now on, even though they may not have agreed with it before the ban came into effect. Why is this so?

The new law in England and Wales dictates that only one terrier can be used to ground at any one time, provided the terrierman has written permission to be on land where game birds are reared and wild birds are preserved for shooting. This presents a dilemma to many. Under normal circumstances young terriers are often entered with the help of an experienced and reliable worker. True, on digs, one could station a youngster nearby, so that it can listen, watch and thus learn, but the law expects the terrierman to do his utmost to flush the fox from its lair, rather than dig it out. Thus the temptation presented to many is to use live traps and enter young terriers using captive foxes put into artificial earths. For one thing, the scent of captive foxes is slightly different to that of a truly wild fox and, for another, they do not have the same fight in them, so artificial entering is of little, if any, value to a novice terrier. If the breeding is right, then a young terrier will enter when it is good and ready (see chapter five for tips on entering youngsters under the new law), despite what the law dictates! So do not use live traps for such purposes, for practices of this nature could easily get all forms of terrier work banned eventually.

Live traps can be successful, but one must check them every day without fail. If one is not prepared to do this, or circumstances do not allow, then do not use them at all. A fox caught in a live trap will suffer a certain amount of stress from being confined, but coupled with a long period of time without water and, once the bait has been eaten, food, it would cause terrible suffering. I know of a horrific case that involved a live trap. These traps are generally about six feet in length and three feet high and wide, but there are a lot of home-made devices that can be quite a bit larger. An acquaintance of mine, many years ago when I was just a lad, obtained one of these home-made affairs and he set it quite close to some old mineshafts that foxes regularly used, a place I worked with my terriers in those far off days.

The trap was set well away from any footpaths and was baited with a dead chicken one of the foxes had killed. The trap success-fully caught sometime soon after, but this wasn't discovered for quite a while afterwards. The chap in question was eager enough when setting it, but somehow he couldn't be bothered making the long walk back every day in order to check it. The trap, in the end, was discovered by someone else and a badger was found caught in the trap, only it was long dead, having starved to death because of having no means of getting to food and water. There was an uproar at the time and the lad in question couldn't go to local pubs for a long time after this, for fear of receiving some eagerly dispensed home-made justice! And the chap who discovered the trap smashed it to pieces so that it couldn't be used again.

Lessons can be learned from such terrible events. When setting traps, it is good to place them in the desired location and then leave them unset for a few days, so that the local fox population gets familiar with the sight and scent of them. Set them well away from areas of public access, well off the beaten track, but in a place that can be easily checked daily. If checking traps involves long walks, then it is unlikely that one will be able to check on it daily, or one could easily talk oneself out of such a walk. So make certain the trap is within a short distance of either your home, or a road, which will make it far more convenient for daily checks. The best time to check is early morning, but a quick look during the afternoon may also be possible for some, for foxes will sometimes hunt during daylight hours and they are especially active in more secluded spots. If, as in this case, a badger is caught, it is simple enough to lift the door, either a guillotine type door that drops down when triggered, or a flap that swings shut, in order to let the beast go free unharmed. Remember, badgers are strictly protected under the law and must be released unharmed if caught in a live trap.

When a trap is left in an area for a few days prior to baiting, the local fox population will quickly accept its presence. If there are dead leaves, or brambles, or any other vegetation that can be placed around the cage in order to give some sort of camouflage, then all well and good, but otherwise do not worry, I have known live traps be successful when placed at a likely location and baited with chicken, rabbit, or some other delicacy that will tempt foxes in, without any camouflage whatsoever. They can be a very effective tool and can be placed almost anywhere. Farmers can set them close to their farmyard in order to catch a chicken thief, or a gamekeeper can set them close to reared pheasants, or a shepherd can place one or two around lambing fields during springtime. Of course, this will not guarantee catching the culprit, for only the use of hounds can do that, but at least there is a greater chance of stopping the unwelcome predation.

These traps are useful in the fight against fox predation, aiding in the battle to control their numbers, but they are most effective when used in an urban setting (see chapter eight). However, despite many foxes quickly becoming trap-shy, some problem foxes will be caught using live traps. When a catch is successful, quickly dispatch the animal so that it suffers as little stress as possible. Do not put it into a drain and loose the terriers, or set it free and then shoot it. Simply shoot it in the head using a .22 bullet gun and its suffering will be ended instantly. Do not shoot through the mesh with a shotgun, for this will only ruin the trap and there is some risk of ricochet too.

Again, I must emphasise the need to make daily checks on live traps and to be determined not to be put off in this. A heavy fall of rain, or some unexpected event may make checking difficult, but, nevertheless, it must be done, for a fox in a trap will suffer to some extent, however minimal this may be, and ending its suffering quickly is the best way of dealing with your quarry. Respect for the quarry we hunt is vital. And, remember, do not be tempted to use this method of catching foxes for the purpose of entering young terriers. If a terrierman is incapable of catching foxes out in their natural wild state, on their terms, then he has no right even considering hunting such a cunning and worthy opponent. Of course, a minority will always turn to such methods, for they always have done, but any self-respecting terrierman would not even consider such actions.

When I first began using terriers to ground, a friend of mine told me of an acqaintance of his who had captured a large dog fox in a live trap and then kept it on his allotment, in order to enter young terriers to their traditional quarry. Foxes in this situation become more aggressive, losing much of their fear of dogs and attacking a terrier at the earliest opportunity. This one-time friend of mine had purchased a Jack Russell terrier and he was keen to try it at fox. He paid his acquaintance a visit down at the allotment, not knowing of the fox kept inside one of the sheds, and was then told all about it. He was not keen on the idea of trying his terrier in this way, but the allotment holder insisted that he did and the terrier was put to the fox. The fox immediately attacked the young dog, but it was bred on traditional lines and cleverly dodged the lunges, while baying keenly at its foe. The allotment holder mocked the terrier for not going in and mixing it, which gives some indication of just how much of an idiot this chap was, and so the youngster was withdrawn and put back in the car. Just how many terriers had 'mixed it' with this fox is anyone's guess, but one can imagine what a miserable life this poor creature had. Although this chap wouldn't admit it, I am sure that it escaped in the end, for, not far from the area where he had an allotment, I came upon a fox that I am sure was that very beast.

I was hunting in the low country and several chickens had been taken from a couple of nearby farms that produced eggs for sale to the public. My hunting partner and I had found quite a few carcasses lying around, quite close to the farm, most of which were partly eaten. On the edge of a field, quite close to one of the farms, is a stone drain from where I have accounted for quite a few foxes over the years. On this occasion Pep, an early Plummer terrier, went to ground at this spot and, before she could begin baying, which was the usual scenario when a fox was found, she yelped in pain as her quarry came up the tunnel to meet her and attacked without warning. Pep was a good little bitch and was experienced at fox, so it wasn't long before she had gathered her thoughts and got herself together, now having figured out the intent of her quarry and dodging the vicious attacks, while baying eagerly and nipping and teasing as the battle raged.

We then began digging, for it was obvious this fox had no intentions of moving, but that dig proved hard indeed, not because it was deep, but because the fox moved every time we broke through. The tunnel was quite large and the fox had no fear of the terrier, so it simply barged into the dog and moved her back a few feet every time we tried to catch it. Eventually, however, with persistence, we did break through and I was able to quickly grab it by the brush and pull it out until I could get hold of the back legs and pull it free of the hole. We at last accounted for what I was certain was the chicken thief and, I am sure, the escapee from that allotment. If one comes across a fox that displays a similar temperament, it is either an escapee from those who have used it to enter young terriers (I must stress that only a very few of the working terrier world would resort to such artificial and cruel methods), or it has come from an urban background where it lost its fear of dogs. Foxes, that is, ones reared in the country and having lived uninterrupted lives in the wild, will usually flee from a dog as quickly as possible. True, in some cases, a fox will find itself trapped in a stop-end and thus it cannot bolt, especially when the terrier is a determined worker, but very often a fox will bolt readily when a terrier is entered. This is especially true when one works silently above ground, giving a fox no idea of one's presence. A terrier is quietly slipped into an earth and one waits silently outside, preferably out of sight of any bolt holes. Soon after, if the fox is not cornered, it will be out of there rapidly and either caught in a net placed over the bolt hole, or is run down by a lurcher, or possibly shot. If a fox comes up to meet its opponent and attacks at the earliest opportunity, then it is likely to have been caught in town and then released into the country, or has been a captive at some stage in its life. In either case, it will usually be live traps that are used to catch these foxes in the first place.

Snaring

The same general rules apply to snaring. If daily checks cannot be carried out, then do not snare. If the land is close to housing estates, or it is regularly used by dog walkers, then, again, do not snare. Do not set snares around pastures where livestock graze either. The one setting the snare must pay attention to detail and set the snare correctly. Only new and unused snares should be set. Once they have caught a fox, then throw them away, for snares must be free running and have a stop attached, in order to allow a fox the chance of escape, but in all honesty a properly set snare will

A well used fox run, a good place to set a snare.

not usually allow this. The best time to check snares is during the early morning, though it is also a good idea to check again during the evening. If lambs are being taken, then several snares can be set around pastures close to the lambing fields, but not actually in the lambing fields. Fox runs are clearly visible to the experienced eye and one should look for reddish hairs caught on a fence which the run goes under, or a hedge bottom, or the run may go along the edge of a field. The run through a field may be a faint track, or even a very well worn pathway, leading narrowly through the grass. Badger runs tend to be slightly broader and far more worn than fox runs, and latrines will be found close to them in places. Never set snares on badger runs, even though foxes will undoubtedly use them.

Despite the best efforts of the setter of snares, on occasion a badger, a cat, or a dog, may become caught in the snare. Being free running and having a stop attached, the snare should do very little damage and one must quickly cut the wire with snippers and set the unfortunate captive free. This is easier said than done. Dogs are usually less troublesome, though a timid farm collie can be a problem. Snaring should only be carried out with full approval of the landowner and one should inform the farmer, gamekeeper, or whoever else owns the land, of the times when snares are being set, in order that pet cats and dogs can be kept indoors during that

Snare set along well-used fox run. 1. Peg holding snare firmly. 2. New unused snare. 3. Hazel, or willow, pegs to hold snare in place.

period, to avoid any accidents. Urban areas are increasingly encroaching on the countryside and snaring should not be practised in this sort of mixture of town and country, for far more cats and dogs are bound to become entangled in the wire. When cats and badgers are encountered, throw your coat over the head and do your utmost to secure the beast until you can quickly snip the wire from around its neck, holding the head down with a pitchfork, or some other suitable tool that will not hurt the animal in any way. If the head is covered, many animals will calm down and be less stressed and this is your opportunity to set it free, though one must act quickly. If you have been successful in catching a fox, then shoot it immediately and put it out of its misery. Foxes do become stressed when caught in snares and that is why snares must be checked regularly *without exception.*

Snares should not be set anywhere near public footpaths, or anywhere where there are wild deer, which does make things a little difficult. Because of the risks involved, snaring is very often a last resort, for, despite one's best efforts to catch a lamb-killing fox, or one that is taking other farm livestock or reared game birds, the crimes continue, even though several foxes have been taken using the lamp, along with the gun, or lurchers, or both, and terriers and lurchers during the daytime. In this situation, snares are another tool one can use in the fight against damaging predation. However, great care and common sense must be exercised when doing this. In fact, one should not snare until shown by an experienced countryman how to do this properly, for setting snares correctly is an art form and a highly skilled business. The Warrener, Pat Carey, runs courses for carrying out fox control, including snaring, as do quite a few other professional pest controllers, so why not enroll on such courses before embarking on the use of snares. The BASC publishes a code of practice. Visit their website and glean as much information as you can. Details can be found at the back of this book.

Another thing to consider is if hounds work the country where snaring will be carried out. If so, then find out on which days there are meets and lift all snares during the time that land will be hunted over, even if an artificial scent is to be hunted. Great care must be exercised and much forethought should go into the practice of snaring. If one cannot be responsible about it, then do not set

Snares are useful where we cannot use lurchers, terriers, or the gun. (The author *(right)* with fox bolted by his terrier)

snares, it is as simple as that. If one does decide to use snares, and they are useful when foxes are lamp-shy and are coming from places where one has no permission to hunt them, or places where one cannot get, such as railway embankments and motorway verges, places that hold surprising numbers of foxes, then make certain that only new and unused snares are set. These should be tied to something solid, like the trunk of a hedge, or fixed to a metal peg that is driven into the ground until it becomes a solid anchor. A hazel twig is then stuck into the ground and this is split at the top so that the wire can slot into it and be held in place. The loop needs to be around eight inches in diameter and stand at a good few inches off the ground, depending on the angle of the run. If the snare is knocked over, then it may need setting a little higher. If it is set too low, then rabbits may knock it over. Where the run comes down a bank, then a height of six inches should be about right. The loop should be pear-shaped. If the weather is windy and rough, then two hazel twigs may be necessary to hold the snare and a little camouflage may be needed in order to cover these from view. Whatever one does, though, some foxes will quickly figure out the danger from snares, especially if they see another fox caught in one. The scent of wire and man will quickly alert a fox of the danger in this situation. The peg must be driven into the ground so that it cannot be pulled up and the wire must be new and unused, not only to allow it to be free-running, but also so that the fox does not snap it.

If the loop is too big, then a fox may get the wire around its body. This will still hold the fox, but this illustrates why it is so important to use the correct tools in good condition, for a fox snared around the middle, should it pull the snare free, or snap the wire, will suffer greatly as it continues on in the wild, greatly hampered as it hunts. When Johnny Richardson hunted the Blencathra Foxhounds, a fox was roused by the pack and, as it headed off across the bleak fell, the Huntsman and Whip noticed that the fox was moving very awkwardly. Hounds soon caught up with their quarry and the hunt servants examined it afterward, finding that it had a snare caught around its middle. A fox in such circumstances must have a very hard time of it and would undoubtedly only survive by taking lambs, or farmyard fowl. So make certain those snares are in prime condition and that the peg is driven solidly into the ground. When snaring, respect for the intended quarry is vital and one must be resolved to carry out this form of pest control in a responsible and highly efficient manner, for nothing less will do.

CHAPTER SEVEN

FOX CALLING, SHOOTING AND FIELDCRAFT

F OXES are incredibly cunning creatures in the main, and anyone who has hunted them for any length of time will no doubt have come to appreciate this fact, but there is one thing that most foxes just cannot resist and that is the squeal of a rabbit or a hare in distress. Foxes are opportunistic hunters and they will quickly respond if the chance of an easy meal presents itself. When a rabbit squeals, very often because it is being attacked by a stoat, or some other predator, a passing fox will quickly react in the hopes of stealing the meal from its rival, which may, at times, be another fox. A quick reaction is usually vital, for a stoat will soon drag the rabbit away, even though it will weigh much more than the stoat itself, and is much bigger in size, and pull it into an enclosed area where its catch is very often safe from being stolen. The hunter of foxes can utilise this natural instinct in order to more easily catch up with lamb and poultry killers, and in order to keep the fox population down to reasonable levels.

This is done using what are known as fox calls, which imitate the sound of a rabbit or a hare, in distress. There are a number of these on the market and they are easily obtained from any of the suppliers listed at the back of this book. There are wooden and metal ones of all shapes and sizes and the cost of these can vary quite a bit. They are useful for both day and night time calling and are very effective, but in areas where foxes are 'hammered' on a regular basis, many of the remaining fox population can become 'call-shy' and actually calling them in to a distance where they can be shot, or taken with a lurcher (all references to taking foxes with dogs, if they are not anecdotes from past experiences, apply to countries outside of England, Wales and Scotland, where foxes must now be shot, rather than taken with dogs), can be very difficult indeed, though not impossible. Varying the call, for instance, may bring results in areas where the fox population is very familiar with this kind of hunting.

Some develop a call of their own by sucking air through their lips and front teeth and this can be very effective in bringing foxes in. This, if you usually use calls, may be one way in which call-shy foxes may be fooled in the future. Another way is to experiment with different calls, such as that of a hare, instead of a rabbit. A Jack-rabbit call will suffice in this situation, for it is the same as the hare. Where a fox ignores one call, it may come running in to another, though very often, even if they do come in, a call-shy fox will do so very cautiously and one may not get them in as close as other foxes. In this case, bullet guns, rather than shotguns, are best used, for foxes can be taken using such guns at greater distances.

The use of calls, both in the daytime and at night, has revolutionised fox control until it has become, in some ways, too efficient. A pest controller, whether professional, or amateur, should aim at protecting farm livestock and reared birds, as well as local wildlife of course, but that does not mean he has a licence to slaughter every fox in the neighbourhood. True, most fox controllers would not even consider such a thing, for their future hunting would be seriously threatened, but some do engage in a 'numbers game'. I have encountered this myself, on a number of occasions. A fox has been taking stock and scores of foxes are killed because of it, whether the crimes have ended or not. Now, I am sure that the majority of those who shoot foxes do so responsibly and with respect for the quarry they hunt, but a minority are more concerned with how many foxes they can shoot, rather than catching up with livestock killers, or simply carrying out effective control.

A friend of mine lives out in the country and he is surrounded by grazing for large flocks of sheep. As you can imagine, there are plenty of problems with lamb-worrying foxes in such places and so control is essential, of which shooting foxes is a very important method. Shooting foxes, in fact, is essential, for, despite the best efforts of terriermen and those who have running dogs which take foxes, or packs of hounds, one simply cannot always catch up with a lamb killer. In this situation, or where foxes live in areas where it is impossible to hunt with hounds, or any other working dog, shooting is vital. But in some areas these shooting folk are out almost every night and are shooting as many foxes as possible, simply because they are in competition with others and the battle is on for who can account for the highest number of foxes. Bets are undoubtedly placed too.

Around the home of my friend, almost every night, all year long, without any observance of a closed-season, are four-wheel drive vehicles with lamps attached which sweep the fields from the narrow country lanes, or dirt tracks, negotiated using these vehicles. Foxes are picked up in the beam and shot using bullet guns. And then those same people are in the pub comparing the numbers taken with great rivalry. My friend drinks in the same pub as this bunch of idiots and he has had a go at them on numerous occasions for their unsporting and irresponsible approach to the shooting of foxes, an approach that will bring growing opposition to shooting in the near future, despite this sort of thing only coming from a small minority. The only trouble is, now that hunting with dogs is illegal in England, Wales and Scotland, this may become a growing problem as more turn to guns for the hunting of foxes!

Shooting safety is of paramount importance, especially in the light of recent accidents that have ended in tragedy, and anyone who takes up shooting, whether it be foxes, clay pigeons, rabbits, pheasant, or any other legal quarry, should join the BASC (British Association For Shooting and Conservation) and should follow their code of practice and the excellent advice given on shooting in a safe and responsible manner. They even run courses that promote this and it may well be worth enrolling. There is not the room in this book to go into all the different aspects of shooting safety, but a few common sense rules should be discussed. But before discussing these, it is important to say that you must make certain that you have written permission to shoot over land and that you are fully licensed to do so.

First of all, guns should be kept clean and in good condition at all times. Shooting in the daytime is fraught with dangers, but shooting at night can present even greater danger to the unwary. One aspect of safety is to know your ground well. This means walking over it during the day in order to become familiar with every nook and cranny. This is especially important when four wheel drive vehicles are used for crossing the land at night, for many have lamps mounted on these and they drive around the country in search of foxes, as well as along country lanes that border these fields. This is a very lazy way of hunting, but it has the advantage of giving the hunter the ability to cover much more ground in one night. The only trouble is, foxes will soon learn to associate the sound of the vehicle with great danger and this form of hunting will create more lamp-shy foxes than does the hunter who carries out his craft on foot, and thus in silence. Electric fences and wire across gateways is a hazard for those who drive around the country, so make certain that the farmer is informed of exactly when you will be on his land and ask if you can take these down for that night, provided, of course, livestock will not be able to get free.

Lamping and shooting foxes is a very effective method of control.

In fact, one should not enter fields where livestock is grazing anyway. If permission is granted, then make certain that, after hunting, all gates are closed and all wire is put back up. If you are having to constantly stop your vehicle in order to open and close gates, then few, if any, foxes will be found, for they will have been frightened off by the noise. Also, inform your local police of your location before going hunting and use sound moderators at night and during the early morning, in order to keep disturbance down, for the local fox population, yes, but also for those who make their homes out in the country.

When hunting using lamps mounted on a vehicle, and this form of fox control is becoming increasingly popular, then it is important to have at least two people on board, though three is an ideal number; one to drive, one to lamp and the other to shoot. A friend of mine often travels over to Ireland where he hunts with a couple of professional pest controllers. They drive around the narrow and deserted country lanes and lamp the fields, using fox calls to bring foxes in closer when they are spotted and then either shooting them, or loosing the lurchers. They don't get a lot of exercise though, for even the foxes that are shot are retrieved by the lurchers, so accounting for foxes in this manner is about as strenuous as a Sunday afternoon drive in the country! But still, it can be a very effective way of taking foxes that are troublesome to farmers, shepherds and gamekeepers. This pair of Irish pest controllers, during more troublesome times in Ireland, have been stopped at night by members of a terrorist organisation and have had to warn their English friend not to speak, as well as instructing him to cover up the guns, which they feared would be taken, showing them the lurchers and explaining that they were looking for foxes. My friend has had some pretty hair-raising experiences while out in the wilds of the Irish countryside during those times when terrorism was at its worst.

It is essential, and this cannot be stressed enough, not to transport loaded guns, either in a vehicle, or whilst walking. If there is a chance of a fox being encountered while walking, then make certain the safety catch is on, right up until it is absolutely necessary to switch it off, when, for instance, dogs have entered a covert and a bolt is imminent. Even then, keep the gun pointing at the ground until it is essential to prepare for a shot. And *never* point the gun at people, or animals. Always be aware of exactly where your companions are, as well as the dogs being used to flush foxes. Always wait for a clear shot too. If, for example, a pair of eyes is illuminated in the beam of the lamp, do not go taking pot shots. Wait until you can clearly see your fox before taking a shot. This will be essential when using shotguns anyway, for a fox must be brought in to at least forty yards if a clean kill is to be guaranteed, but this also applies to bullet guns, which can kill foxes at far greater distances. Some use a lamp mounted on a rifle. If so, then use the rifle in this way when it is unloaded. Do not go pointing a loaded rifle all over the countryside in search of foxes. Once a fox is caught in the beam, then switch it off, give a few calls and then load the gun. With the safety catch on, pick the fox up again and call it in further, until it can be shot and killed cleanly. Alternatively, use the lamp to find your fox and then switch it off and mount it on the rifle, before calling it in and shooting it. Of course, this is necessary when lamping alone, but if you have a companion, one can shoot, while the other lamps. When bushing foxes using dogs, make sure that the fox is well away from the undergrowth before shooting, for a dog could easily be injured if some stray shot penetrated a spot where it was hunting. And, if a dog emerges on the brush of a fox, do not even think of taking a shot. Let it run on for another day. Remember, it is just as important to have a clear shot, as it is to have a clean shot that will kill your quarry instantly.

Another good reason for walking over land during daylight hours is to find which areas have public footpaths running through them in order that these places can be avoided. It is surprising how many folk are out at night and I have, on quite a number of occasions, whilst lamping, come across people walking through the country at night, no doubt taking a short-cut home after an evening's courting, or a night out at a pub, or a club. Areas where public footpaths are found should be avoided at all costs. Do not take any chances, even during the early hours.

Observation is essential when shooting and one must make certain that there is a safe backdrop to a shot. Never shoot a fox standing on the top of a hill, or with woodland as a backdrop, for one never knows if someone is in that wood. Also, make certain that there is no wire in the way that could cause the bullet to be deflected. A clear and clean shot is essential. A friend of mine, Rob, was deer stalking in the Highlands and he raised his rifle at a stag that was standing with a wood behind it. He was inexperienced at this game and his more experienced companion quietly said, 'Make sure of that shot. There is a road running behind that wood.' Needless to say, Rob quickly dropped the rifle and wiped away a few beads of sweat that had appeared because of the thoughts of his carelessness and what might have been! A safe backdrop is essential. Shotgun pellets will not travel too far, but a stray bullet can go on for surprising distances and carelessness can easily lead to a fatality. There is no room for carelessness when shooting, whatever the game involved.

The new law in England, Wales and Scotland means that foxes must now be shot after being flushed with dogs. This can be a very effective form of control, for foxes, in the main, will live above ground for most of the year and it is not too difficult to find them sleeping in undergrowth, using good hunting dogs that will keenly search out a skulking fox. Let not the terrierman who is used to earthwork scoff at the idea of terriers working above ground in this manner. A large covert is a real test for any working terrier and some are so dense that the twisting passages below are very similar to an earth anyway. The guns should cover all exits by standing around the place, while trying not to be too conspicuous, and the dogs should then be entered. Working silently will almost guarantee a quick bolt and guns should be at the ready as soon as the dogs disappear beneath the dense foliage. Once a fox is flushed, the guns must wait until it is well clear of the covert and into an area where there is no danger of spreading shot hitting either their fellow guns, or the dogs doing the flushing. Sometimes a terrier, lurcher, or hound, whatever the breed used, will emerge almost on the brush of the fox and give chase. In this situation, a shot is impossible, for the dog would be either injured, or killed, and so the fox must be allowed to run on. If the dog catches it, in England and Wales, as long as there was no intent, then, according to DEFRA, there will be no action taken, should the matter be reported, but I must stress that this has yet to be tested. I cannot guarantee that such things will not bring about a prosecution. All I can say is that several foxes have already been killed by accident in this manner and no prosecutions have resulted, for the police seem to have adopted a common sense approach to the new law on hunting.

At the time of writing there is much debate about the amount of wounding that results from shooting. It is claimed that shooting causes more suffering than does hunting and common sense tells any reasonable person that this is undoubtedly true, for hounds either catch and kill their quarry, or it escapes. With shooting, wounding is always a possibility, especially when one considers that very often a decision and a shot has to be taken within just a few short seconds, but the pro-hunting lobby must not try to discredit shooting in an attempt to save their way of life. Shooting is an essential form of pest control, particularly fox control, and is incredibly useful in situations where livestock is being taken. True, wounding will occur at times, using both shotguns and bullet guns, but that wounding is kept to a minimum when experienced guns are employed.

If a farmer picks up a shotgun, or rifle, and *occasionally* takes shots at the odd fox causing him problems, then yes, wounding is going to occur far more often, but in the hands of an experienced shot, wounding has got to be less likely. A scientific research paper dealing with shooting was published in May of 2005, which conducted tests on life-sized paper foxes, both still and moving targets, and dead foxes, using shotguns and rifles. Basically, .410 shotguns caused far more wounding than twelve-bores and bullet guns. No.6, BB and AAA shot was used during both day and night shooting and rimfire and centre-fire rifles were used, all at different distances. The study found that experienced shots missed far less targets, though they stated that the wounding rate remained the same. It was found that bullet guns caused less wounding and that, up to forty yards, both BB and AAA shot was very effective when using shotguns. Wounding is far more likely after the forty-yard range has been exceeded, but then we knew that already.

These tests may prove that wounding occurs when shooting foxes, but country folk already knew this to be true, that is why gun packs implemented a policy of using the hounds to hunt down any wounded foxes in order to end any suffering resulting from such wounds. Thanks to the new law in England, Wales and Scotland, that is no longer lawful and so wounded foxes will get away and die long lingering deaths from starvation, or infection. This bill to ban hunting was supposed to be about animal welfare, but more suffering and more deaths will occur due to this new law. Not that shooting should be banned. There are many who would like to see this happen, true, but a ban on shooting should not be brought about because of research that proves wounding occurs when shooting foxes. As I already stated, we knew of this before this research was published and humane steps were taken in order to end the suffering of injured individuals.

The only problem with such research is that it was conducted under artificial conditions. Although the paper foxes were moving targets, they were not real foxes. Also, they were moved along gaps, which only allowed the shooter three or four seconds in which to take aim and fire. This is undoubtedly the time one has on occasion, but very often, especially when calling foxes in, one has more time to prepare for a shot. If a fox is spooked, when being called in, sometimes it can be stopped by a quick squeak on the call. When it turns back to look, then the gun has the opportunity to account for it, so yes, at times only a few seconds is available, but not always. Tests conducted under artificial circumstances can only give some idea of what occurs. The shooting I have witnessed, in the vast majority of cases, has been unbelievably effective and death has been instant. Many, for instance, use a heavier shot than No.6 and I have seen foxes dropped instantly using such shot. .410 shotguns should never be used for foxes, for they are just not powerful enough. They are ideal for shooting rats and many use them on rabbits (even then, a .410 will wound more rabbits than does a twelve-bore), but should not be used for the hunting of foxes. Nor should air rifles be used in this capacity. I know of someone who recently shot a fox using a .22 air rifle and he dropped it instantly. The pellet had gone through the ear and into the brain, thus death was instant, but that was a lucky shot and 99.9 per cent of such shots would cause wounding, some of which would be life threatening. Not that he was out after foxes. He was stalking rabbits when a fox emerged right in front of him and he took a shot. He was lucky in that he hit a particularly weak spot and dropped it, but the outcome could have been very different.

A common sense approach is necessary when shooting and one must quickly decide which shots are likely to kill, rather than injure. If a fox is wounded and gets away, it is illegal to hunt it down in order to end its suffering in England, Wales and Scotland, so, in theory, one must leave it and allow it to suffer a terrible death that may take up to two weeks, or longer, to occur. In this situation each individual must search his or her own conscience and then decide on an appropriate course that would quickly end the victim's suffering. I am not encouraging anyone to break the law, but each individual must decide how to act in this sort of circumstance and if one chooses to hunt the fox and finish it off, then that is their own decision, for many just cannot stand by and see an animal suffer. The anti-brigade may label those who hunt and shoot as cruel, but, in fact, for the vast majority, the opposite is true. A quick death is always aimed for and shooting, in the main, produces an instant death rate, no matter what studies conducted under artificial circumstances say to the contrary. Although shooting folk respect the rights of each individual to hunt if they so wish, they do not want to see their way of life discredited unjustly in order to preserve hunting with dogs. Both forms of fox control have a necessary place and both are very effective, though hunting with dogs, of course, is far more selective than shooting. The hunting community must not feel that they have exclusive rights to the killing of foxes, for that wouldn't work at all.

Much of our country cannot be hunted nowadays, due to busy roads, railways, motorways, growing urban areas etc, so shooting is absolutely necessary. Also, in big woods especially, foxes can so easily escape hounds, so shooting is incredibly effective in these areas too. There is plenty of room in our countryside for both hunting and shooting and the combination of two dogs flushing to waiting guns will prove very effective in many areas (though not in large woodland and forestry, where a pack will be needed to drive out foxes from such sanctuaries). The view of 'exclusivity' expressed in the world of foxhunting with hounds has been just one aspect that has been so distasteful to the public in general. This undoubtedly has its roots in the days when anyone who shot a fox was considered a 'vulpicide' and was often driven off the land for his 'crimes'. If he was a farmer, his tenancy would be revoked, or if he was a farm worker, he would quickly be out of work and evicted from his cottage. Although things are not like that nowadays, there is still an element of this within the foxhunting world.

I was recently ratting in Nottingham when a pack of hounds

Mark Brennan's deerhounds with foxes taken on the moors.

drew the wood we were hunting. A ferret was to ground and rats were bolting all over the place, but the terriers were distracted by hounds milling around. The Huntsman then appeared and bluntly asked what we were doing. We had full permission to be there and before we could speak he said 'I 'ope yer not f——n' foxin' '. Needless to say, Carl and I were not amused and the Huntsman was sent on his way with a 'flea in 'is ear'! This attitude of exclusivity is one that has made the world of hunting with hounds unpopular in many circles and has created powerful enemies over the years. Another aspect of this is the self-governing rule that, should a fox be hunted into another hunt country and it goes to ground, it must be left to run another day. Why? If fox control is the aim, then why should a fox be left in this situation? Surely it is essential to account for a fox, even under such circumstances, especially if it is a problem fox. Not all Masters, though, abided by such customs.

Nicholas Spink was one-time master of the Bilsdale Foxhounds of North Yorkshire, which were once a trencher-fed pack. The hounds were excellent hunters and often ran foxes for hours and into the hunt countries of neighbouring packs. On one occasion the Bilsdale ran a fox into the Hurworth country, running it to ground at Welbury Whin, where it was dug out with the terriers. The Master of the Hurworth heard of this and promptly wrote to his neighbour, complaining of the man's breach of hunting customs. In typical blunt northern fashion, Spink soon replied to the letter of complaint he had received. He simply stated 'We allus dig – Nicholas Spink'. Obviously, Spink ran an establishment based on fox control and not 'sport', though undoubtedly his hunts provided plenty of sport for the followers. Hunts today must focus on control and the reasons that make it necessary should remain at the forefront of campaigns to see hunting return in England and Wales in its more traditional form. Hunts established in countries where hunting remains legal, must focus on improving public image by highlighting the necessary and selective role hounds and terriers play in controlling a predator that can cause serious harm to the livelihoods of farming communities and wildlife. This is essential if bans are not to follow in these places.

Bolting foxes from earths to waiting guns is another effective form of control and it is important to work as silently as possible when carrying this out. If a fox is alerted to the danger outside, it may not bolt and that could present difficulties in England and Wales, especially if restrictions are put on the amount of time a terrier can be to ground. What one should aim for is to bolt the fox as quickly as possible. I am not a shooting man myself, but I have ferreted and carried out terrier work for guns on many, many occasions and I enjoy this form of pest control. A terrier will soon become experienced enough to mark an earth as occupied, or otherwise, and one should keep it on a lead while quietly allowing it to test the scent at each entrance. If it shows interest, then a fox is likely to be home, if not, then move on elsewhere, if the terrier can be trusted that is. If a mark is given, and this is displayed by the terrier looking into the hole and wagging its tail furiously, or by digging at the entrance, then get the guns to stand in likely places, out of sight of the bolt holes, but well placed so that a clear and close shot can be employed once the fox bolts. And all of this must be carried out as quietly as possible, lest Reynard be alerted to the goings on above ground. Once in place, loose the terrier and a bolt should occur soon after, though this can take up to twenty minutes or so, depending on the size of the earth. If it is large, then a fox may give the terrier the run around for a while, before bolting, or it may decide to head for a stop-end and stay and fight it out. So always fit a locator collar when using terriers to bolt foxes to waiting guns. This is advisable when bushing foxes too, for a terrier may get to ground if an earth has been dug deep inside the undergrowth.

Derek Webster carries out a lot of fox control on keepered land and Paul Stead, the terrierman for the Pennine Foxhounds, accompanied him around a shoot in the north of England. One of Paul's terriers marked a fox to ground and so the keeper stationed himself at a likely spot, before the terrier was loosed and entered. Gem went to ground and soon after a fox bolted, but the keeper wasn't able to take a shot, for it popped into another hole nearby. Gem then emerged and followed her quarry to ground. She bolted it again a little later and once more the fox popped into another hole before a shot could be taken. Gem was quickly on the scene and followed her fox to ground yet again, bolting it soon afterwards. Unbelievably, this unadventurous fox did the same thing again and was once more followed to earth by Paul's terrier. On the fourth occasion, however, Reynard bolted and ran for it, being shot and killed instantly by the expert shooting of the gamekeeper.

I was out hunting a valley on the outskirts of Rochdale and Noel, a shooting friend, stood in likely places as Ghyll worked through the gorse and bramble bushes. Even without camouflage, if one stands still against a backdrop of woodland, or hillside, rather than sky, foxes will very often not see you until it is too late. Sometimes they do not see you at all and die oblivious of your presence. Ghyll was working a large gorse covert when a fox bolted and casually walked towards us, completely unaware of our presence. Noel took aim and fired with his twelve-bore shotgun and the fox was dropped instantly, not even having heard the bang of the gun. Controlling foxes in this manner, as long as clear and clean shots are taken, is very humane indeed and few woundings will occur under such circumstances.

Earth-stopping for fox holes remains legal, but exactly why this should be so when hunting with hounds has been banned in England and Wales, is rather a mystery. True, now that flushing foxes from undergrowth and shooting them is growing in popularity, one could carry out earth-stopping in order to ensure foxes are above ground and thus, in theory, in covert. This, however, is not always the case. Foxes will sleep the daylight hours away in a number of varying locations and are not always found in undergrowth. Brambles, bracken, gorse and deep heather are the favoured couches of the vulpine race, but they will also choose other sites, such as among hay bales, rushes, crops, under farm buildings and even churches. When I was a kid (and not too choosy where I hunted), I more than once had a terrier to ground, rather illegally it has to be said, under a country church! They have even been found in trees before now. Brian Plummer, in his book, *The Fell Terrier*, tells of a fox that was found in a tree by John Parkes while out hunting on a keepered estate, and this is not an isolated case.

I believe earth-stopping is unnecessary when flushing foxes to waiting guns. Foxes are usually found above ground anyway and many seem to be reluctant to go to ground. This has been the case on many occasions in hilly and mountainous districts where earth-stopping is virtually impossible, when a fox has been hunted for hours and for many miles, yet has shown no inclination to go to earth. Earth-stopping is now unnecessary and impractical where hunting with hounds is banned. I believe it was already unnecessary anyway, except in the case of badger setts, or other impossible earths, which can be used to escape hounds when hard pressed (stopping badger setts is now illegal in England and Wales). Earth-stopping originated with those who were only concerned with providing a sporting day out, not fox control, so one questions exactly how necessary it is in this day and age when control is all-important to the image of the hunting scene.

One effective way in which foxes can be taken is to wait some-where close to a well-used run that a fox is using in order to attack farm livestock, or reared game, or the nest of a wild bird. Camouflage is useful in such situations, though some think it unnecessary. Foxes, if one sits or stands still with a background of trees or hedges, or any other suitable backdrop, will very often not see you until the very last minute. On numerous occasions I have had foxes run towards me and pass by as close as a few feet away, without seeing me at all, when my terriers have been bushing, or when I have been out with hounds. But still, wearing camouflage gives the shooter that extra edge and can mean the difference 'twixt success and failure. One must be still and patient, allowing the fox to come within range of a clear and clean shot, before taking it. A large fox was causing problems at a lowland farm and a friend of mine, Noel, was called in to deal with it. A fox run has been used by countless generations of foxes, which leads directly to the farmyard, and he waited close to it one evening. Sure enough, as the light began to fade, a fox came ambling along the run, intent on paying a visit to the farm again, and Noel, using a .22 bullet gun, dropped it instantly once it was within range. Methods such as this are incredibly effective and waiting by a run that is known to be used for access to a farmyard, or to lambing fields, will often mean that the culprit is caught, rather than an innocent fox passing through. Sometimes, of course, more than one fox is responsible for losses and quite some time may have to be spent controlling problem foxes in one location. In such circumstances, it is good to use a variety of methods.

If, for instance, some foxes have proved lamp- and call-shy, then baiting an area close to the farm and waiting nearby may well bring positive results, though great patience will be needed in such circumstances. One could build a small hide for cover, or simply use a hedge, or the cover of a woodland, or stone wall. If using a hide, build it a good few days before using it, in order that the local fox population comes to accept it as part of the landscape. There are all kinds of scents available on the market these days and a masking scent can be used. Obviously, when lamping foxes, or waiting for them to come to you, during night or day hunting, it is important to work into the wind in order that foxes coming into you cannot detect your scent, for that would see every fox in the district disappear in minutes and carrying on would be pointless. The wind will take your scent away from the area you are working in this way, but there is always the danger of a fox coming in behind you and catching your scent, so masking scent is useful for covering yours, just in case this should happen. Sprayed all around the back of where you are hiding, it will mask your scent and, hopefully, keep you from being detected. Bait an area during the afternoon in order that your scent is blown away by the time foxes are out, though one must keep an eye on the bait, lest crows, or magpies, or even a farm dog, try stealing it.

Keep your eyes and ears open. If crows and magpies are kicking up a fuss, then a predator is around. Of course, this could simply be a cat, but it is likely to be a fox, so be prepared and load your gun in readiness. Movement should be minimal and noise non-existent at this time, for, as the light fades, foxes are likely to be out and about. As well as baiting, a lure scent could be put down. Also, there are small tape players that can be bought that have speakers and various fox calls can be played, in order to draw in your quarry (lure and masking scents, and calls, can be obtained from suppliers found at the back of this book). There is a chance that no foxes will come in until darkness has well and truly set in and so, if foxes in that area are lamp-shy, one can use either a red filter on the lamp or night vision binoculars that can be used to keep an eye on the baited area. Once the fox is feeding, flick on the lamp and shoot as soon as a clear and clean shot is available. In this situation, it is best to have a second person present, in order for one to use the night vision and flick on the lamp, the other to do the shooting. Also, whilst looking for foxes, both in the lamp, or when using night vision, be observant and make certain there are no farm dogs knocking around, or people, for some folk do cross the countryside at night. It is possible for separate sets of lampers to meet up at night too, so take great care when shooting at night, as well as in the daytime.

Night vision is very useful when hunting fields full of cattle. Cattle can fuss around someone using a lamp, so night vision means one can sit quietly and look for foxes, without the cattle knowing you are there. But I must stress that you must not shoot in such places. Where there are cattle, use a lurcher for catching foxes. Call the fox in to as close a range as possible and then flick on the lamp, while immediately loosing the lurcher. Do not slip lurchers on foxes that are close to hedges, walls, or woodland, for Reynard will easily get away and one can create yet another lamp-shy fox. Also, when using lurchers, make certain that they will return as soon as the lamp is switched off. If a dog follows a fox through a hedge, or over a wall, then it could so easily be knocked down on a road, or fall over a cliff edge, or into a quarry, thus severely injuring, or killing itself. Again, when either shooting, or using lurchers, it is absolutely necessary to know your ground well and so avoid potentially dangerous places.

When calling foxes in to the gun, especially when hiding in amongst a hedge, or some other backdrop, or when shooting from the back of a four-wheel drive vehicle, a tripod is most useful for allowing a completely steady hand when taking aim and firing. In this way it is much easier to keep the sights on the fox as it moves in towards the waiting gun. Tripods, if you do not have a very steady hand, are excellent tools that aid greatly a sure and clean shot. When using these handy tools, it is best to have a partner doing the lamping, though a lamp mounted on a rifle is also very useful when working alone.

Another method of hunting foxes using either lurchers or guns, is to find a dead sheep and wait nearby. Note from which direction the runs come in to the carcass and then wait downwind of them, preferably with camouflage clothing helping you to blend in with the background. Good fieldcraft is essential when hunting foxes, for they are constantly on the lookout for danger and, should you slip up in any way, you will usually ruin the hunting for that night. If fox runs come from all directions, then choose a spot downwind

A dead sheep stripped bare by foxes. Waiting near a carcass is a good way of shooting them.

of the carcass and spray masking scent to your rear. Hopefully, this will prevent detection from any fox that comes in behind you, though success, when this occurs, cannot be guaranteed. Sheep carcasses will often attract quite a number of foxes and finding one, especially on the moors, or in mountainous districts, may prove rewarding, though, again, this is a game of great patience and attention to detail, when it comes to fieldcraft, must be observed.

Sometimes though, despite all of your preparations, things can go wrong and your hunting, day or night, can be ruined in no time at all. We had been clearing foxes on a sheep farm and had enjoyed mixed success. I found a fox family in a drain at the foot of the moors and quickly and quietly left the site, in order to plan a way of taking them. I hate to kill cubs, but sometimes, when lambs and other livestock are being taken, it is necessary. This was during the early days of my career as a hunter of foxes and I still had to learn much of the cunning of foxes. Roy and I met up with Gordon and Phil early on the Saturday morning and it was decided to bolt the foxes and Gordon and Phil would shoot them with their twelve-bore shotguns. We began by working a nearby quarry, which bordered the land where lambs were being taken. The terriers checked the rockpiles eagerly, but no foxes were at home, so we headed off the moor and made our way to the drain. The terriers entered and fox scent and remains of prey were abundant, but the vixen had cleverly moved her family elsewhere and we never did catch up with them.

That same springtime we were asked to lamp the farmer's fields in order to catch up with the culprit. When tackling livestock predation, it is best to try a variety of methods during both day and night time hunting, in order to maximise your chances of success. On this occasion, we decided to use the lurcher, rather than the gun, though we baited the area with woodpigeons Roy had shot that very afternoon, in order to attract foxes to the empty fields where we wanted them, rather than in the fields full of lambs. Combined with the fox call, we knew we had a very good chance of taking a fox or two that night. The pigeons were put down long before darkness set in, just to allow our scent to fade and hopefully disappear completely, before darkness enveloped the land. And then we headed to the farmhouse in order to let the shepherd know

Derek Webster with
May and Ranger and
a fox taken on the
lamp.

of our presence. And that, I guess, is when things started to go wrong.

Two other friends, Paul and Dave, wished to come along and Roy and I agreed, though we were a little worried about the famer's reaction to having four people on his land. He was a dour chap and never seemed happy, even though Roy and I had been carrying out good, effective pest control free of charge, and not only tackling the local fox population, but also reducing rat and rabbit numbers too! We called at the farm during that Saturday evening, just to let him know that we were on his land and to make sure that it was okay to have Paul and Dave along with us. He was as grumpy as ever, maybe a little more so at having been disturbed on a Saturday night after a long working day had ended, but he agreed, for he knew that his flock needed protecting and, after all, it would cost him nothing.

He walked out to the farm gate with us and suddenly erupted, once he had seen Dave's milk van. 'Is this chap a milkman?' He asked angrily, pointing at Dave with a trembling hand. Before we could answer, Dave was getting out of the van. 'Do yuh get yer milk from me? No yuh bloody-well don't, do yuh?' He turned to Roy and me, both of us standing there open-mouthed, shocked at his totally unreasonable reaction. Dave too, was stunned into silence and just stood there, looking stupid. 'Am not 'avin' another milkman on maa land. He would be welcome if he bought maa milk, but he don't, so am not 'avin' 'im 'ere,' he continued, before turning and storming off back to his cosy fireside, no doubt lamenting the state of things; the injustice of having to live in a world where many milkmen didn't buy their milk from him! We couldn't believe what we had just witnessed, so we drove to the other side of the valley and walked onto his land once pitch-blackness had set in. Normally I would comply with the wishes of a farmer, but back then I was young and more than a little stubborn. I was also rather put out by such an unreasonable reaction after he had agreed to Dave and Paul joining us, so I made them stay and they followed us onto the fields. The night was pitch-black and windy and so we were hopeful of taking a fox or two that night.

We walked in silence and always into the wind. I flicked on the beam for the first time that night and it was good to see that our baiting had worked. A fox was picked up in the first sweep of the lamp. It was quite some way off, but still, it provided an opportunity of displaying to Dave and Paul just how effective a fox call can be. I reached into my pocket for the call, though this wasn't really the sort of place one should keep such instruments, for this was my hunting coat and all sorts of things went into those pockets, including dead rabbits and a fox brush or two. I put the squealer to my lips and blew as hard as I could.

Unfortunately, some sort of debris from my pocket must have lodged inside the call, for the sound emitted was more akin to a duck being strangled, than a rabbit in distress. And there lay a lesson quickly learned. It is just as important to keep your fox call in clean and good order, as it is your guns! Lamping foxes and calling them in is a tense and exciting form of hunting which has plenty of adrenaline rushes. Things were that tense that night, after the raging farmer and the first fox picked up in the beam, that the strange sound of that squealer sent us all, all that is except Dave, who took hunting, not to mention life in general, a little too seriously, into hysterical, uncontrollable fits of laughter, made worse by the shaking of the beam and by our attempts to keep silent and not frighten off our quarry.

We needn't have bothered though, for our fox was now long gone, no doubt terrified of that strange sounding creature which had emitted that unnerving sound. Still, we carried on until we came to a deep gully, intent on success. Stopping there, I scanned the field in front and yet another fox was in our sights. The gully, however, prevented Merle from having a good run at his prey and so we had to cross it first, the wind masking any noise we would make whilst doing so. Roy climbed over the fence, but misjudged his footing and he just fell away from us like a statue being toppled, and landed on top of a large bramble bush in the bottom, which just kept him out of the brook that was full of the waters from the spring rains.

That capped it. Paul and I fell about in heaps, trying all the while to stifle as much as possible of the uncontrollable laughter which was made worse by the vision of Roy slowly falling backwards, his eyes wide, his face pale, with fear of the unknown, unable to be banished from our minds. All the while, Dave whispered angrily at us to shut up, but he just made things worse. Even Roy joined in the laughter, now that he had realised all was well, the springy, though a little prickly, undergrowth cushioning his landing. As a formality, though with a spark of hope, I flicked on the beam, but we all knew well before doing so that it was a pointless exercise, for every fox in the district would be in the next county by now, after all of the noise we had made. It was time to head for home, for no self-respecting fox would show itself again that night; of that we could be certain.

Shooting foxes is a very effective method of control and can be carried out during both day and night hunting, and using a combination of fox calls, bait, dogs for flushing from undergrowth and terriers for bolting them from earths. But I would once more like to highlight the need for responsible control and not slaughter. Large numbers of foxes can be taken in very short periods of time when shooting foxes, so it is important not to kill too many in each area. The numbers game will only see fox numbers drastically reduced until they become scarce in our countryside. This attitude was displayed one night when a friend of mine accompanied a shooting enthusiast on a lamping trip. He shot seven foxes that night and, on the way home, a dead fox was lying in the road, freshly killed. The shooting man got out and picked it up, putting it with the others. Why? Was it so that he could show his mates and tell them he had killed eight foxes, rather than seven? Who knows. If this was the reason, then it shows how dangerous this attitude of killing for the sake of numbers is. Control, not slaughter, is the aim of any true countryman.

The hunting ban presents another problem in England and Wales in particular. If foxes are being shot in the springtime because of taking lambs and possibly other farm livestock, there are going to be cubs that will fall victim too, due to the death of the vixen, or even both parents. If the cubs are weaned and a barren vixen, possibly two barren vixens in some situations, are helping to feed them, then survival is most likely, but if no other foxes are helping to rear a litter and both parents are killed, or the vixen is killed before the cubs are weaned, then death is assured for the whole litter. Before the ban, one could find the breeding earth, if a nursing vixen was killed, and the cubs dealt with by loosing a terrier into the earth. Now, unless on land where written permission is granted in order to protect reared game, or wild birds preserved for shooting, that act would be illegal and the law thus dictates that these cubs should be left to starve slowly to death. If the cubs are mobile, then one could wait above ground and shoot them when they emerge, using a sound moderator, but this is no ideal answer, for cubs may not yet be emerging into the outside world. Again, the hunter of foxes must do his utmost to end suffering quickly and conscience will undoubtedly find a solution to such a problem!

CHAPTER EIGHT

URBAN FOXES

THERE are two schools of thought regarding urban foxes; one says they are a nuisance and that control of their numbers is necessary, while others say they are a delight to have on the streets and that they do no harm at all. Foxes are predators and a harmless fox does not exist. In Dartford, Kent, a couple took their baby to hospital after it had been bitten by a fox. There have been other reports of foxes attacking family pets, including dogs, cats, rabbits and guinea pigs. In fact, while I was at the Coniston country fair during 2004, I met a chap there who had a Jack Russell with him. He was from Wolverhampton and only a few days before a fox had jumped over his back yard wall and had attacked his terrier. He heard her yelp and went out to investigate. He found his dog bleeding from a wound to the head, but there was nothing else to be seen. A few minutes later his neighbour knocked on his door and told him that a large fox had jumped over the wall and bitten the dog, before leaving. Those who claim that urban foxes are harmless are kidding themselves and belong to the same brigade who preach that foxes do not attack lambs and chickens.

In urban settings, more so than out in the country where foxes are often hunted and thus kept on the move, foxes pack and any predator that packs, presents a certain amount of danger. Urban foxes lose their fear of man and dogs to a large extent and this in itself can be dangerous. Reports in Edinburgh suggest that over two dozen pets are killed annually by urban foxes, while a few more are attacked, but survive. This, of course, refers to reported cases, but I would estimate that it is safe to double, possibly even treble, these figures in order to get a real idea of how much damage foxes can do in an urban setting. However, despite all of this, many enjoy seeing foxes out on the streets of towns and cities and it can be said with certainty that they are here to stay. At the time of writing, rabies is a growing problem in Germany and it is feared that foxes

A chap from Wolverhampton with his Jack Russell that was attacked by a fox in his back garden.

could be affected in France, which presents a danger of rabies getting into this country via the Channel Tunnel, so some sources say. If rabies did get into Britain and foxes became infected, then the urban population would present a great threat to public health and safety. I fear that it would be all out war against urban foxes if rabies did break out in this country.

Urban fox populations originated as towns and cities started to grow, particularly after World War One, but more so once the building boom began during the 1950s. Of course, foxes have always hunted through the streets of villages, raiding bins etc, but only during brief nightly visits. Once towns and cities began growing and more and more countryside was swallowed up, and thus more territory of foxes, they began moving into the streets and found suitable dens among churchyards, back gardens, tips and any spare land that could be found. Railway embankments are also a favourite haunt and the tram system around Manchester holds a good number of foxes. In fact, if one watches carefully during the spring months, one may see cubs playing on the embankments at any suitable spot, such as where brambles grow in profusion.

Foxes will prey on birds and rodents, especially rats, in an urban setting, and thus they help to keep the numbers of vermin down to some extent, though they will also prey on family pets such as rabbits and guinea pigs with equal enthusiasm. Stray dogs also take pets from hutches, so foxes are not always to blame, but family pets do make up part of their diet in an urban environment. Although some claim they are harmless, urban foxes can make a nuisance of themselves in several different ways. They can dig up parts of a garden as they hunt around for insects and uncover worms. They mark their territory regularly and this 'spray', as well as the scats (droppings), is rather pungent to say the least. They also raid bins and split open bin liners to get at the contents inside, though wheelie bins are fox proof when not filled to overflowing and thus problems with raided bins are now becoming less common. Foxes will scavenge leftover food on the streets and at the back of take-aways and restaurants and this food source makes up quite a large part of their diet. In fact, if it were not for such food sources, especially now that many bins are fox proof, many foxes would either turn to killing and eating pets, or starve to death.

Cats are sometimes attacked by foxes, especially when they are in a pack situation and food is scarce, though sometimes they will attack them even when food is plentiful, no doubt in order to eliminate the competition. Cats can be very fierce opponents though and can cause injuries that get infected and eventually kill the fox, so many avoid a confrontation, though some do become rather adept at cat killing and avoid serious injuries while doing so. Again though, not all savaged cats have been attacked by urban foxes. Stray dogs are certainly to blame on some occasions. Like foxes, few stray dogs will tackle a cat on their own, but in a pack situation of even two dogs, they become bolder and often kill cats whenever the chance arises. Having said this, some foxes do kill cats, no matter what some say to the contrary.

Another problem with urban foxes is the risk of the spread of disease which they carry. Distemper and mange are the two main diseases foxes will spread, so it is vital that dogs and any other pets that can catch distemper, be inoculated at the earliest opportunity. Mange is more of a problem among urban foxes, simply because they live in more cramped conditions. Foxes will often pack and disease spreads much easier in this sort of environment. Out in the countryside foxes are hunted regularly and, where hounds have been used, the sick and the weak have been removed, very often before they could infect other foxes. And thus outbreaks of disease are often stopped abruptly. In an urban setting though, things are really quite different. Foxes are allowed to proliferate and where there are plentiful food supplies, and generally there are with scraps of food being available when thrown on the floor or even put in an open bin, where foxes will easily get to it, there, there will be found larger numbers. And, where there are larger numbers of foxes, there will be more outbreaks of disease. In an urban setting it is impossible to set up a programme that will eradicate many of the sick population and thus disease continues to spread and break out. When hunted by hounds, sick, old and weak foxes, the main carriers of disease and those most likely to spread them, will fall victim on many occasions and thus diseases are often kept in check. Urban foxes are not controlled and thus disease will break out more frequently, and do far more damage, in this kind of environment.

Some councils have put into operation fox control measures on occasion, employing marksmen to shoot them at night, using sound moderators so that the public are not disturbed, but you will find it impossible to get them to admit it, due to the current climate of 'political correctness'. Few of these programmes will be ongoing enough to have any impact however and so the urban fox will continue to be a problem. Of course, marksmen travelling around at night and shooting foxes does present a certain amount of health and safety issues and live traps would be better in this situation. Foxes are quite easily caught in live traps in urban settings, simply because they will scavenge almost anywhere and are so familiar with human scent that they take no notice of it anyway. Simply baiting live traps and then shooting the captive foxes, would be a very effective way of carrying out control of their numbers in a safe manner.

Live traps are so effective that some are catching them in this way and are then taking vanloads of captive foxes out into country areas where they are released and become a severe problem to local farmers. Urban foxes live mainly on scavenged food and so hunting out in the countryside is an alien art to them and thus they have great difficulties surviving. And a hungry fox is a problem fox. One can easily tell an urban fox loosed into the countryside. For one thing, many of them are sickly, weak specimens and some are covered in mange. Another sign of an urban fox is one that has no fear of dogs, nor man. I have come across a few during hunting trips and the terriers have caught them easily, simply because the fox has just stood its ground, without any fear whatsoever. Urban foxes are familiar with pet dogs in towns and cities, many of which will turn tail and run if a fox shows any aggression. And thus they view all dogs in this light and get a shock when hounds, lurchers, or terriers catch up with them in a country setting that, after all, is completely alien to an urban dweller. Urban foxes should be put down when being controlled, not released into the countryside where they will prey on the easiest options available – lambs and farmyard livestock. Many lamb killers have proven to be released urban foxes in very poor condition. Many of these foxes live on refuse tips and they feed largely on rats and almost inedible waste. Mange is rife among these fox populations and releasing such animals into the countryside only puts the wild population at risk. True, some foxes do eventually recover from mange, but the majority will die slow, agonising deaths due to the severely scratched skin becoming infected. A terrible death often follows an outbreak of mange and those thoughtless idiots who release them into the wild are only causing more suffering.

Some have blamed foxhunting folk for catching urban foxes and releasing them into the country, in order to restock dwindling supplies for hunting. This is ridiculous. Released urban foxes are very quickly 'chopped' by hounds simply because most are sickly creatures and they do not have a natural fear of dogs, so they do not, or, indeed, cannot, make a run for it as would a country fox in fine condition. So hunting folk have no desire to hunt poor specimens such as these. The whole exercise would be pointless, for urban foxes released into the country do not provide good hunts. I am not certain who exactly is behind this capture and release programme, and it would be pointless speculating, but one thing I do know, it only causes harm to both the urban foxes released, and the native country foxes too.

The most recent released urban fox I caught was one day when I was hunting in the Pennine hills. We were hunting through a deep valley when Fell scented something among the reeds. I quickly spotted what it was; a fox, which just stood there while Fell hunted its line for quite some time, until he eventually arrived at the clearing and attacked his fox with gusto. I ran over and finished off the unfortunate creature and it was in very poor condition. It hadn't made a run for it because it had no fear of dogs or man, which immediately tells of its urban background. It was in poor health too. This was January and the fox should have filled out by this time, but it looked like a twelve-week old cub. Its coat was thin and lifeless, its brush in very poor condition. It was almost weightless too and had obviously been struggling to feed itself. I feel that we did the poor beast a favour that day, but this would have been completely unnecessary, had the idiot who released it not done so. As I said earlier, live traps and shooting the captives should be the favoured method for control in urban settings, or marksmen should be used, if the councillors deem it safe to do so. In this day and age, though, with many of our streets being inhabited by people even into the small hours, the use of marksmen in such settings does present some safety issues.

Along with true urban foxes, which spend all their lives on the streets, there are also fox populations that live a semi-urban, semi-country lifestyle and these will dwell in both settings. I was once called out to hunt down a lamb killer and the culprit, it seemed, was coming from woodland surrounding the pastures which were on the edge of town. On the edge of the woodland, however, were new housing estates, the pastures where I used to poach rabbits as a kid having been bulldozed and built upon a few years earlier. We found nothing in the woodland and could only guess that the fox was living under a shed, or a garage somewhere among the large cluster of unsightly houses. Noel and I searched high and low for even an earth, but none could be found, so he called the culprit in on the lamp and shot it instead.

Derek Webster, while hunting on a keepered estate, once dug a fox that was fitted with a collar. Not a collar that was being used in order to track the fox for research purposes, but a dog collar for domestic pets. This may have been an urban fox that had escaped from someone who was attempting to rear it as a pet, which had been caught and released into the country before the collar was

A hard dig through chalk after Mist had killed a semi-urban fox

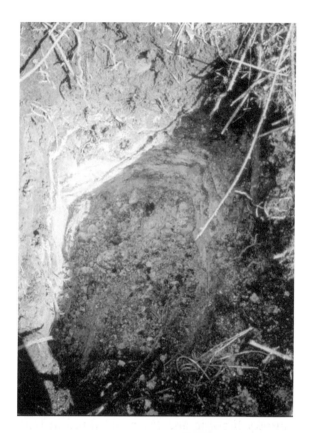

The result of the dig!

noticed, or it may have been a fox that had been injured and taken in by a do-gooder, having escaped later, once its injuries were healed. It is difficult to say, but one thing is certain; foxes do not make suitable pets. They smell rather badly and always retain a certain amount of wildness about them. They are also destructive – just one of the reasons why urban foxes can be a nuisance.

I find foxes that live a semi-urban/country existence, like urban foxes proper, lose quite a bit of their fear of dog and man. A terrier to ground on such a fox will often have difficulty bolting it, for they are simply not intimidated in any way, though they may soon change their outlook when a harder terrier is put to ground. I was out bushing rabbits with my terriers in a narrow valley that is surrounded on both sides by housing estates, when Mist disappeared. I searched for her and eventually found her baying keenly inside a dug-out rabbit hole in the middle of a bramble bush. I had not fitted a locator collar, simply because I know this area very well and we were not near any of the known fox earths. However, a fox had recently dug into this place, probably in order to catch its prey, initially, but finding the place suitable as a home once it had done so.

I hoped the fox would bolt, so I stood back and waited. However, the fox was reluctant and Mist worked it hard, but, eventually, after half an hour of 'persuasion' it bolted. It was a large dog fox, unmistakable with its broad head and magnificent brush, and it just looked casually at me (I was standing just a few feet from it) and then ambled off in rather a laid-back fashion. Had Derek Webster been there with Rocky, or Noel with his gun, we would have taken it easily, but as it was it escaped unhindered. I expected Mist to follow soon after, but she didn't. She carried on baying and it was obvious that another fox was home. This fox was also reluctant and chose to stay and make a fight of it. That was a big mistake, however, for soon afterwards Mist began whining – an unmistakable sign that a terrier is trapped and cannot get out. She had killed the second fox and its carcass was undoubtedly blocking her exit. Mist stands off and bays, generally, but has grown harder during her later seasons and will now kill a fox that will not bolt.

I blocked the entrance, just in case Mist managed to get free, and headed home, in order to return the rest of the terriers and to pick up digging tackle. I could have entered another terrier with a locator collar on, but I doubt it would have stayed to a dead fox anyway, and probably not even long enough to get a mark on the box, so I decided to dig her out using skills I had developed long before using such devices. I decided to follow the hole for a short while, just so that I could get an idea of the area in which she was lying, for sound can be very misleading inside an earth. I eventually dug down to a fork in the tunnel system and her whining was definitely coming from the left side. I then put a long stick up this tunnel in order to get some idea of the direction it took, and then put my ear to the ground in the area I estimated her to be. Sure enough, I could hear her somewhere below this spot, but the sound was faint, indicating quite a deep dig. Also, this was on a steep bank, so I had to take out huge amounts of earth in order to keep the back of the dig, as well as the floor, level. If I failed to do this, then the sides of the dig would be unstable and I would be left, as I went deeper, with very little room to work in. The deeper the dig, the more of an area will need to be dug out.

I cleared the brambles first and then had to cut through thick roots. After this, the going was easy enough, being mainly made up of soil, but I soon hit compressed chalk and this was no joke. It took me an age to dig through and the going was very slow indeed. To make matters worse, I hit a twisted mass of rusting metal, which had to be cleared away before further progress could be made. The trouble was, it was starting to get dark and I would have to spend quite a bit of time digging around this obstacle in order to remove it. So I blocked up the entrance after putting my coat and a bowl of fresh water inside that I had fetched with me when returning with digging equipment. I would leave her for the night and I hoped she would be waiting for me at the entrance in the morning.

I returned at first light and removed the blockage, but there was still no sign of her. She barked and whined when I called and, sure enough, she was stuck fast in the same place. I got stuck in straight away on that cold, frosty morning and was soon down to my T-shirt, sweating with the difficult going of the dig. I soon removed the metal and managed to cut a large square out of that hillside, shifting tons of earth, until, at last, Mist could be heard very clearly. I knew I was very close and so took my time, lest I break through and injure, possibly even kill, my terrier. A large stone was on the edge of the dig and I knew I must move it in order to make

Mist, after tackling the semi-urban foxes.

further progress. As I did so, some of the earth suddenly fell in and I was through, opening up the hole directly behind my terrier who was drawing her prize towards me. She had killed a barren vixen inside that earth and she was in surprisingly good spirits, not wanting to leave her prize behind. But she needed food, water and a good clean up, as well as treatment for her bites, so I got her home as soon as possible and returned to backfill once my bitch was fed and bedded down. This reluctance to bolt, or run from covert, I have experienced on numerous occasions when encountering urban and semi-urban foxes. Barren vixens will sometimes help raise cubs, so I guessed there was a litter somewhere nearby that had been fathered by that large dog fox Mist bolted during the previous day.

Fox control in an urban setting should be carried out by the proper authorities, but there are things householders can do in order to protect their pets and/or their babies and young children, though I must stress that it is very rare for a fox to attack a human being. I have known lads hunt urban areas with terriers and lurchers and they have been incredibly successful too. One lad I know used to take part in organised hunts in Bradford, West Yorkshire, using terriers to bolt and flush foxes to lurchers, on tips and any spare ground encountered, and they took numerous foxes in this way, but this form of hunting is now illegal and probably was then, if permission wasn't granted from the landowner. Make certain that you report any incidents involving fox predation, or destructiveness, and ask your local council about its policies for control. If there are none, then demand that something be done about a troublesome situation. One may be 'peeing against the wind', however, when broaching such a subject, so do not have high expectations when complaining about nuisance foxes. One way in which to avoid attracting urban foxes to your home environment is simply not to feed them. Some put food out regularly and then find the foxes being destructive around their garden and neighbouring gardens. Also, make certain they cannot get to food intended for other wildlife.

Rubbish, especially leftover foods, should be put in fox-proof containers such as wheelie bins. Dustbin lids must be secure, so do not overfill your bin. Another tip is to clear wind-fallen fruit on a daily basis, for foxes will eat fruit just as keenly as they will eat meat. Pets and other livestock, such as those found on allotments, need to be kept secure with fox-proof netting. Cages should be well constructed and in good condition. If the wood is flimsy, or rotten, a fox will quickly get through it and kill the occupant. Also, normal chicken wire will not keep a fox out, nor will that plastic stuff that is about 'as useful as a teat on a boar', so purchase a cage with strong mesh, preferably welded mesh, which will prevent foxes from chewing their way into the cage. Also, cages can be put out of reach of foxes, or they can be put inside a shed or a garage, where your pet will be much safer. Some think that having a dog around the place will help deter foxes, but that simply isn't true. The chickens at our local hunt kennels are taken fairly frequently, despite there being about twenty couple of hounds only yards away! Commonsense precautions must be taken when living in areas where urban foxes dwell. After all, despite its beauty and its cuddly looks, the fox is simply a predator whose instincts are geared and finely tuned for survival and so anyone who keeps pets and livestock in an urban setting must be on guard against their predatory antics.

LIST OF SUPPLIERS

Arthur Carter, P.O. Box 198, Lytham St Annes, FY8 5XH.
Tel. 0845 370 3113. Fax. 01253 796775.

Johnson Fieldsports, Unit 5 Ireland Close, Off Fan Road, Staveley,
Chesterfield, S43 3PE. Tel. 01246 477666.

Attleborough Accessories, Morley St Peter, Norfolk, NR18 9TZ.
Tel. 01953 454932. Fax. 01953 456744.

Target Sports of Bolton, 486 Halliwell Road, Bolton Lancs,
BL1 8AN. Tel. 0870 0607331. Fax. 0870 0607332.

Foxshot Night Vision UK, Borderside, Southwick Road, Wickham,
Fareham, Hants, PO17 6HX. Tel or Fax. 01329 832364.

Deben Group Industries Ltd, Deben Way, Melton, Woodbridge,
Suffolk, IP12 1RS. Tel. 0870 4422600. Fax. 0870 4430110.

BIBLIOGRAPHY

Foxhunting on the Lakeland Fells Clapham (Tideline Books 1989, first published 1920)

Lurchers and Longdogs E G Walsh (Standfast Press)

Foxhunting Jane Ridley (William Collins Sons & Co Ltd 1990)

The Patteradale Terrier Seán Frain (Swan Hill Press 2004)

Hunting – The Facts (BFSS, now The Countryside Alliance)

The Fell Terrier Brian Plummer (The Boydell Press 1983)

The Council of Hunting Associations is publishing a code of conduct for the use of birds of prey in conjunction with hounds.

INDEX